A RELATIONSHIP IN CHRIST

A RELATIONSHIP IN CHRIST

"BE INTRODUCED"

KAL CZOTTER

authorHOUSE®

AuthorHouse™
1663 Liberty Drive
Bloomington, IN 47403
www.authorhouse.com
Phone: 1-800-839-8640

Published by AuthorHouse   04/25/2013

ISBN: 978-1-4772-7149-0 (sc)
ISBN: 978-1-4772-7148-3 (e)

Library of Congress Control Number: 2012917450

NEW INTERNATIONAL VERSION®
RIGHTS AND PERMISSIONS GUIDELINES
(USA & CANADA)

The "NIV" and "New International Version" trademarks are registered in the United States Patent and Trademark Office by Biblica, Inc.®

I. Policy for Use of the NIV® text

A. General Statement

The NIV® text may be quoted in any form (written, visual, electronic or audio), up to and inclusive of five hundred (500) verses or less without written permission, providing the verses quoted do not amount to a complete book of the Bible, nor do the verses quoted account for twenty-five percent (25%) or more of the total text of the work in which they are quoted. This permission is contingent upon an appropriate copyright acknowledgment. (See section II below.)

B. Use of NIV® text beyond the limits of section A above requires written permission.

1. Commercial use:

    Commercial use means the use of any product offered for sale, lease, rental or barter on any level, or use in advertising. Rights and permission to quote from the NIV® text in media intended for commercial use within the U.S. and Canada may be granted by Zondervan Publishing House, 5300 Patterson SE, Grand Rapids, MI 49530. Requests for these rights and permissions should state: (1) the exact portions to be quoted, (2) the medium in which those portions will be quoted, and (3) the purpose and distribution of the medium.

2. Non-commercial use is defined as the opposite of the definition of commercial use given above and generally means free provision of the medium in which the NIV® text is used. Most usage by local churches would fall into this category. Rights and permission to quote from the NIV® text in media intended for non-commercial

use may be granted by Biblica US, Inc., 1820 Jet Stream Drive, Colorado Springs, CO 80921-3696. Requests for these rights and permissions should state: (1) the exact portions to be quoted, (2) the medium in which those portions will be quoted, and (3) the purpose and distribution of the medium in which those portions are quoted.

II. Acknowledgment and copyright notice

Any quotation from the NIV® text must include copyright notice and acknowledgment. The form the acknowledgment takes will depend, in part, upon the medium in which the quotation is used.

A. Written Use: Use whichever of the following notices is most appropriate:

1. The following notice may be used on each page where material quoted from the NIV® appears:

   Scripture taken from the HOLY BIBLE, NEW INTERNATIONAL VERSION®. NIV®. COPYRIGHT © 1973, 1978, 1984, 2011 by Biblica, Inc.®. Used by permission. All rights reserved worldwide.

2. When (NIV®) is marked at the end of each Scripture quotation from the NIV®, the following notice may be used on the title page or reverse thereof of each copy:

   Scripture quotations marked (NIV®) are taken from the HOLY BIBLE, NEW INTERNATIONAL VERSION®. NIV®. Copyright © 1973, 1978, 1984, 2011 by Biblica, Inc.®. Used by permission. All rights reserved worldwide.

3. The following notice may be used on the title page or reverse thereof of each copy:

   All Scripture quotations, in this publication are from the HOLY BIBLE, NEW INTERNATIONAL VERSION® NIV® Copyright © 1973, 1978, 1984, 2011 by Biblica, Inc.®. All rights reserved worldwide.

The "NIV" and "New International Version" are trademarks registered in the United States Patent and Trademark Office by Biblica, Inc.®. Use of either trademark requires the permission of Biblica, Inc.®.

B. Visual and electronic use

This category includes videos, films, slides and overhead transparencies. Electronic denotes the use of an interactive computer. Quotations from the NIV® text in visual and electronic media must include whichever copyright notice from section II-A is most appropriate on (1) the product (the medium itself), and (2) products wrapper or packaging, and (3) in an acknowledgment section, if one exists.

C. Audio use

This category includes cassettes, compact discs and similar media. Quotations from the NIV® text in audio form must include whichever copyright notice from section II-A is most appropriate on (1) the product (the medium itself), and (2) the product's wrapper or packaging. If the NIV® text is used as the lyrics for a song, you must obtain permission from Biblica US, Inc. prior to production of the same.

D. Church use

Any use of the NIV® text by a local church in or on non-commercial media such as bulletins, orders of service, bulletin boards, posters, overhead transparencies, recordings of worship services (for which a small handling fee may be charged), or similar materials use in the course of religious instruction or services at a place of worship or other religious assembly, requires the following notice at the end of each quotation: (NIV®). Audiocassettes may include (NIV®) acknowledgment on label only.

III. Additional information about NIV® rights and permissions

For rights and permissions not expressly granted or referred to in this document, or for an explanation of any provision of this document, write to: NIV® Permissions, Biblica US, Inc., 1820 Jet Stream Drive, Colorado Springs, CO 80921-3696. Persons requesting rights and permissions not expressly granted in this document should state: (1) the exact portions to be quoted, (2) the medium in which those portions will be quoted, and (3) the purpose and distribution of the medium in which those portions are quoted.

Any commentary or other Biblical reference work produced for commercial sale, that uses the NIV® text must obtain written permission for use of the NIV® text.

BIBLICA US, INC.
1820 Jet Stream Drive, Colorado Springs, CO 80921-3696
Telephone: 719-867-2740
Rightspermissions@biblica.com

A RELATIONSHIP IN CHRIST

My Affirmation

The main tools I use for coping with life are faith; hope; family; community; the churches' guidance; belief in God, Jesus and the Holy Spirit; mental health support and true spiritual guidance through the Holy Bible. When I started this book, I was truly ready to serve. Prior to my vision, I was trying my hardest to please God, for the Trinity had ended all my addictions in my life. It was done by God's hand! I really wanted to serve and do something big for God, but our God does not need our help. He can do all things expressly without humanity's help. Just as I said, He can do all things on His own! As I prayed in frustration, I prayed that I might have a purpose in God's immense plans. I prayed hard, and I prayed for years.

And one night after waiting and waiting and waiting patiently, I had a dream and Jesus was in it. The setting was dark, and Jesus was running around, chasing a dragon. The dragon was flying up and down and side to side and all over the place. Then Jesus stopped and walked up to me and said,

"Be enlightened and enlighten others." When I woke, this phrase was in my head. As I rolled out of bed, I could see Jesus chasing the dragon in my head. I can still see it. A few nights later, a week before Easter of 2012, I had another dream, but this time I was writing. I was writing sermons for many pastors and then handing them out. When Jesus appeared, He gave me a pad of paper and told me to write sentences on top of sentence and to put a plus mark in front of every sentence; and at the end of the paper, there were to be no minus marks in front of the sentences. If so, the page would have to be discarded. As I woke up out of my dream, I went to the computer immediately and started writing. Every day after that, I have been filling this book with pages—minus for a lie and plus for the truth. I have not discarded any pages by the grace of the Holy Spirit. Amen.

As I look back over the months I have seen God's plan since I have been enlightened by truth, I can see that there's nothing I can do for God that He can't do. But through His grace, He has given me a chance to share in His work, to work with Him, to have a true relationship with Him and to truly be a part of His life. I am truly blessed on all sides to be able to have the Holy Spirit talk and write to you all, through God's power. When I say "God will bring you to where you belong," pray and have faith in this remark. Please look to share, look to serve, and look to be a part of God's immense plans; may God give all His people the blessing of grace, for all glory goes to God.

Amen.

DAY OF MY BAPTISM

15 April 2012

Baptism is a religious ceremony in which water is used as a symbol of cleansing one from sin. Some churches today baptize by sprinkling or pouring water over a person. Baptizing is a sign that our sins are washed away and that Jesus has taken us to be His own. In baptizing a person, one has accepted Christ's Spirit, the Holy Ghost; a life in community with Christ; and the church. When we initially give our hearts to the Lord, we receive forgiveness of all sin through Jesus Christ's name. Baptism is a pouring out of the Holy Spirit to flesh. Through a new lead to a cleansed heart and soul, otherwise known as new birth, the Lord asks us to believe and be baptized; so it is an act of obedience toward Christ. That one has faith in the Lord and through divine assistance, one makes the decision in their heart to die to sin and live for Christ. Amen

I and another lady met at the church, we sat down and we gathered around Steve, our pastor. He started by welcoming us, and he told us about baptism and about what it meant to be baptized. After we finished listening, we gave our testimonies and told each other why we needed to be baptized. After we drove to Murine Lake on Highway 99 in Squamish BC, I and a lady were baptized in the early spring waters of the lake. I felt a sense of well-being and peace in my heart. It's good to know that I'm home with my family, and I can't wait to start my life. I have died to sin, and I have declared to everyone that I am living for Christ.

15 April 2012

Praise the Lord. Amen

A RELATIONSHIP IN CHRIST

Parable

When one is starting out to gain faith and to have a good foundation in Christ, it is like a family that is going to start a fire in the rain. First the family will create the fire pit where the fire will dwell (an open heart and an open mind) and then they will set out the rocks around the pit (Christ will offer His love and protection). By this time, they will seek the wood (seek God's Word) in order to create the fire (the Holy Spirit). They do this to make the heart and mind complete for their fire (the Holy Spirit). Once the wood (God's Word) is spread out in full view and put in its place, it truly is the heart of the fire. At this point, the father will light the fire and create a flame like no other, bright, awesome, and brilliant. As the fire begins to burn, the rain (doubt) may fall on it, trying to wreck all the family's work, but if the family has built the fire well and stokes it with the proper components (love, faith and hope), the fire will not go out and nothing can stop it from spreading. The family will succeed and share its warmth among others and among themselves.

Praise the Lord. Amen.

HOW BELIEF CAN OPEN A DOOR

We can't be sure that we have something worth living for unless we have something to die for. This readiness to die for our beliefs is evidence to ourselves and to others that the love we receive from God, Jesus and the Holy Spirit is eternal. Jesus is the Way, the truth and the Life, and through the power of Christ, we receive the Holy Spirit (Holy Ghost). Jesus is our Lord of lords and King of kings; He is our Alpha and Omega, Beginning and End. He is our Shepherd, "Teacher," one Messiah and Son of God; He is the Lord. He was beaten, hung on the cross and died for our sins; He was buried in a tomb, and on the third day, He rose. He walked the earth for several days, and many people saw Him and gave praise. His gospel has lived for over 2000 years; He is our Saviour and our Redeemer. God, being our Creator and our Father, forever was and forever will be. He loved the world so much He gave His only begotten Son, and through belief, we are united with the Father, the Son and the Holy Spirit. Belief is the start to embracing the happiness that comes through

God's grace, we are to receive the grace that is abundantly supplied in the person of Jesus Christ, His Son.

This in turn leads to a life that is not self-seeking but a life that is selflessly seeking after the will and purposes of God the father. So in all one might come to Christ and be saved, be born again and through

obedience, he or she will turn from sin and repent. In this write-up, I am going to share the message of belief as well as the Glory of God and how one can have a true and gratifying relationship in Christ.

The Holy Spirit is truthful, honest, loving, peaceful, humble, kind, compassionate and patient. It also gives strength, hope, faith, courage, confidence and self-control. After time you will receive treasures such as devotion, wisdom, knowledge, understanding, victory, honour, and most important love. These are all gifts given from the light and are worthy of existing in every man and women for your future and mine.

So is there anything that we can acquire to make people know and love God with all their hearts and minds? I feel the answer is no. It is a choice for you and for God. Remember that God is sovereign as well. Nothing says that God will make us love Him, but He does not wish to see us perish.

God sent His only Son to be with us in body and in spirit, so He will make Himself known to each one of you. Just keep your eyes open.

God is love; whoever lives in love lives in God and God in him. In this way, love is made complete among us so that we have confidence on judgment day. Or do you think of actions such as being rebellious; being consumed in jealousy or living a cold-hearted life? Or do you have a body with no self-control? Or are you quick to anger? Or do you even have no control of your emotions at all? God asks us to let killers be killers, liars be liars, and thieves be thieves; but the punishment is death or being dead in your transgressions.

So look deep in your heart and mind, as deep as you can go, and ask what is worth dying for; worldly position or even feeding a habit? I feel the answer is no! Men and women should be free and truly motivated through their work and offers of positive expressions. I pray we all are far from oppression and close to our families. Believers will be forever creating, nurturing, preserving and protecting. Days will go by, and you will become more secure in your faith and belief. This is what the Trinity (Father, Son and Holy Spirit) asks from us: Just believe.

To start, here are some shared values that are worthy of residing in every man and woman alike:

honesty	peace	purity	guidance
patience	caring	security	selflessness
love	integrity	diligence	tolerance
kindness	trust	hope	conscientious
fairness	honour	industrious	knowledge
balance	truth	discipline	freedom
creativity	equality	brotherhood	awareness
faith	dedication	co-operation	dignity
perseverance	character	leadership	
individualism	justice	courage	
compassion	respect		
understanding	charity		
responsibility	empathy		

I find the most important ones in this list are faith, honesty, integrity, truth, respect, empathy, a sense of discipline and, above all, love. This is a list of our gifts from the Holy Spirit. In our future, we can walk tall and upright, knowing that these values reside in us that our values align with God's values. As believers, we pray to God to help us not to sway side to side but to walk straight and stand firm in our belief. I know that a good tree does not produce bad fruit. When I was in my young adult life, I was motherless and fatherless; I was selling drugs and living on the streets, but as a child I was close to God. Day after day living in darkness, I hid from God, but He never hid from me; He was always there. One day, instead of running, I faced Him and accepted His wrath. I gave Him my heart and repented; He redeemed me and brought me out of the murky waters. Once that happened, I no longer could lie to myself. I put my life in God's hands; I began the journey through the book of life, the Holy Bible. My life truly started, and my choice to walk with Jesus became devotion. When I look back, I truly see that our Lord God was there all along. Now it is six years later, and I am a man, a man with full endurance and full of faith and hope. I have entered my future saved, baptize, and born again. I am living within a relationship with Christ, close with God; and I am Gathering the fruits of the spirit. Every day I am maturing in the spirit and becoming sanctified by Christ through the living word of God.

Amen. Praise the Lord.

BOOK 1

A RELATIONSHIP IN CHRIST

Book 1

1

The Lord has quenched my thirsts;

my life is like free-flowing water that is not dammed up;

there is much room to grow.

When life runs aground, the Lord God gives way to a

beautiful clean river,

which leads to more water sources, clean and alive.

God was pure, God is pure and God will be pure forever

and ever; this is concrete.

Set these words securely on your heart.

The Lord yearns to see you succeed in bad times and good;

He gives treasures such as strength, faith and hope.

Brothers, sisters, I pray that God blesses you with

knowledge, wisdom and

understanding, for these are the treasures of kings.

When wisdom came to me, it came as discipline;

I pray that you all see God's

sovereignty.

Knowledge is acquired by reading the Bible,

and growing in knowledge will have

great benefits for one's future; Praise the Lord.

I find in our age that understanding is the hardest to acquire,

for the Lord's thoughts are above all humankind and

human thoughts

are perverse,

selfish and initially without understanding.

The Lord is the giver of all these gifts.

How much greater and awesome is the

Father than the child? Amen.

A RELATIONSHIP IN CHRIST

Book 1

2

I speak to the Lord in the morning;

during the day I walk with Him.

I confide in the Lord in times of need.

The Lord is my Father; He loves me and wants to see me

succeed.

The Lord is pure in heart and mind;

through Him all things can be done.

At night I am alone; the day has passed and the Lord

comforts me; and I am

safe.

When I lay my head, I speak to God; He hears my case,

my worries, my thoughts and my dreams.

I am not alone; I am in the presence of the Most High.

I am comfortable in His presence;

I yearn to make Him proud.

And I love the Lord.

Jesus is His name. Amen.

A RELATIONSHIP IN CHRIST

Book 1

3

I Praise the Lord as I open my eyes; I greet Him.

The day is full of things unknown;

I am secure in the Lord and am willing to face the day in

faith.

When turbulent water arises, the Lord's Prayer is in my

heart and on my tongue.

I praise God and look back on what He has done: my life

has been saved,

spared from the cords of death and addiction.

My identity has been renewed.

The Lord has given me back my dignity.

The Lord has given me peace on all sides;

all praise and worship I give to God.

His heart is pure and good.

He leads me down a straight path, so that my heart might

be right with His.

I forgive myself, and the Lord forgives me as well.

He is full of mercy.

So repent to the Lord and follow the commandments.

And fear God for He does not wish to see us perish.

Amen.

A RELATIONSHIP IN CHRIST

Book 1

4

Life has been hard, the Lord knows.

When I was a child, I'd cry myself to sleep, the Lord knows.

I was away from my mom, the Lord knows.

I was hit as a child, the Lord knows.

I was also bullied as a child, the Lord knows.

The Lord gave me strength to go to my mother's house;

the Lord was there.

When I was 13, my mom lost hope, the Lord knows.

I and my sister got broken up and were put into foster care;

the Lord was there.

I became lost and fell into drugs, the Lord knows.

I dropped out of school and sold drugs, the Lord knows.

I went off on my own path and fell away, but the Lord was

still there.

When I was 25, I needed the Lord; He came with open arms.

I am 30 now, I am back in church and have a good

relationship with Jesus.

I am finishing my school, live on my own,

I am free from addiction and I am baptized in the Lord's name.

I am being fully sustained by the Lord

I have been born again.

I have been adopted into God's family.

So pray for strength, pray for self-control and pray for courage.

And, most importantly, just have a real relationship with

Christ,

for He is the Most High.

Halleluiah!

Amen.

A RELATIONSHIP IN CHRIST

Book 1

5

The addiction was strong; I had been ensnared.

My life was treacherous and dangerous;

my clothes they divided among themselves;

liars, cheats and murderers sat at my table.

Prostitutes and wayward women tried to take my life.

My friends set snares for my feet.

Evil men sought my life.

"Lord, Lord," I would say.

"Please help me," I'd pray.

"For this is poison I drink" in my defense I begged "please I

don't

want this cup."

The streets were pitch-black;

at night there was no rest.

The shadows have come out; they dance on the walls.

By day, the mountains melt, and by sight, the base is far away;

the poison has made me ill.

Lord, I know You are there to help me to stop my sinful
ways.
Sin has overtaken me like a fox in a rattlesnake's den;
I had lost my self-control.
For the Lord is my strength, my rock, my salvation, my
fortress, my deliverer!
Please come quickly to lead me from temptation.
Help me to not sin.
Help me to change my life.
Help me, my deliverer.
As I gave my heart to Jesus, I read His gospel; I said to
Him, "my heart is Yours."
Father, Son and Holy Spirit, come into my life;
renew me, restore me, and save me, Oh Lord.
You have given me what I need.
I worship You with all my heart, I praise You with my
tongue and
I boast about You among the people.
You have sustained me and pulled me out of murky waters
and have brought me into a transparent state of mind.
Lord, I want to climb your mountain,
learn Your ways and gather Your faith,

that I might one day stand at the peak of Your Holy

Mountain.

Holy, Holy, Holy is the Lord, merciful, forgiving and just.

Amen.

6

The Lord is my salvation;

His heart is righteous;

I hold close to His Word.

My heart is zealous for His affection,

and I yearn to do His will;

I am a part of His life.

The Lord's sovereignty and awesome power

bring tears to my eyes.

I find joy in times of trouble,

for the Lord is good and pure at heart.

He builds up the poor

and gives security to the old.

All who believe in Jesus will reside in His presence.

I say, live to see His face

and to make Him proud.

Amen.

7

Our security is at the foot of the cross and is made complete

through our

obedience to God.

Secureness is to the one who sows the field,

works the ground

and waters the crops,

for one will reap what one has sown

and eat from the harvest.

Each is satisfied.

The Lord wants us to succeed.

He yearns to see us grow.

We are His crops.

He says that all who have thorns at harvest time will be cut

down and thrown into

the fire.

So ask the Lord to mend you,

that you may be secure on judgment day,

the day of the Lord's harvest.

Amen

A RELATIONSHIP IN CHRIST

Book 1

8

The Lord's houses

have many corners

and many rooms;

they are filled with many hearts from every race;

they spread out over the face of the earth.

The Lord Jesus is the head.

His foundation is secured,

held together by belief upon the Father, the Son and

the Holy Spirit.

The Sabbath is the churches' day holy and righteous;

a day to rest,

to worship,

to gather

and to give tidings;

with the purpose to share each other's belief,

to learn and to listen to God's Word,

to pray for one another,

to sing praise to God,

to unite in community

and to introduce non-believers to Christ;

for it is a home to all believers

and a refuge for people who come to Christ.

It is a place to unite the body of Christ, His people;

that we may learn what His and our gifts are and gather

spiritual confidence,

that we may share the Lord's teachings across the world

and that we may glorify God with all our hearts, in all we do.

The Lord is a bride to the church,

and He loves it until the end of time.

Amen.

A RELATIONSHIP IN CHRIST

Book 1

9

I intend to enlighten you,

open your mind,

broaden your horizon;

because the Lord has opened my mind

to loving myself,

to loving others;

that is the key: love one another.

Ask God for a clean heart

and seek a clean mind that you may have confidence on

judgment day.

Take away all detestable images from your sight

and perversion from your heart; and, in turn, your heart

will not be disturbed.

For your heart is a watchtower and has full view of the mind.

The Lord sees all things and is judge over all, men and

women alike;

His thoughts are pure without flaw.

The Lord's heart is awesome and patient, and it is filled
with illuminating love.
When singing in worship, have a clean heart that your
mind will not be clouded;
worship with a loving soul.
Perversion is like a weed that consumes your mind;
it gathers strength and chokes out the good and the pure.
A perverted image is like a soiled sheet that constantly
shows itself.
Respect God's authority and life will go well;
if one shows disrespect for His authority,
it will bring a rebellious heart
and one will have to face the consequence.
Wait upon the Lord;
have patience,
pray for patience,
pray for understanding,
that your heart may be settled.
Anticipate the day of the Lord's coming
through waiting patiently one will see the mystery of God's
plan.
The day of the Lord will come.
Have patience; do not give up.

"For, Lord, I have faith in You and Your sovereignty."

Deep in my heart I know that the Lord wants to see that we

all succeed.

So whom do you truly believe in?

Whom do you truly put your faith in?

Whom do you truly put your heart into?

God, Jesus, and the Holy Spirit should be your answer;

they will bring you to where you belong.

Just have faith, patience, and hope,

but most of all have love

and it will all come to pass.

Amen.

A RELATIONSHIP IN CHRIST

Book 1

10

The Lord will be there when my ears grow deaf,

when my eyes grow dim,

and when my legs grow weak.

My body is but a shell.

I hope in the Lord, for His healing touch,

that my heart does not give out.

I know my body will fail me,

for this is inevitable.

I am secure; I know the Lord well be present

when all this comes to pass

and my body goes to the grave.

The Lord will watch over me,

and He will bring me to where I belong. Amen.

A RELATIONSHIP IN CHRIST

Book 1

11

The Lord has given us the gospel.

My heart is faint.

It beats for the Lord.

Lord, please give me a person who comes in Your name.

I yearn to share Your word.

Lord, Your name is on my forehead.

I boast of Your works to all the people.

Lord, You have made me an exile among the people.

I am alone in the land of the living;

I wake and look for your people.

But they are not found,

except for in Your house.

The people say, "I don't want to listen" or "I don't believe;

leave me alone!"

Truth is far from them.

And perversion and lack of self-control reside in their

rebellious hearts

and replaces God's grace.

I know that the Lord cannot force us to know and love Him,

especially with all our hearts and minds,

for the Lord does not wish to see us perish.

Remember God is pure.

He wants to see us succeed.

So come all,

be refined,

be forgiven,

be set free from sin

and give your heart to Jesus and repent.

We are all in the land of decision;

be wise and the Lord will lead you.

Do not become like the self-righteous bunch

that thinks they are blameless and that are full of pride.

The Lord asks us to be humble and live in humility,

be slow to anger and forgiving,

be patient and merciful with one another;

He says, "Love one another

and give good gifts."

The Lord has brought us the gospel,

for Jesus died on a cross.

He was buried, and on the third day, He rose.

He walked the earth, and many people saw Him, and

gave praise. After giving instruction to His disciples, He

ascended in spirit to sit at the right hand of God, the

Father, to have full authority and sovereignty over all flesh.

The Lord is the giver of all spiritual gifts,

for He is pure and righteous.

Whoever is filled with pride may the Lord have brought low.

Whoever is on high and self-righteous—I pray that the

Lord shows them their sin

and humbles them.

For every man and women who walks the earth has been,

will be, or is in sin,

but Jesus came to redeem His people.

Praise the Lord, for He makes us blameless

restores our dignity,

forgives our sin,

strengthens us,

gives us hope and faith,

enlightens us with wisdom, understanding, and knowledge

sets us on a path,

walks with us,

carries us,

protects us.

That we my worship the Lord

sing to Him,

praise Him,

and glorify Him, for this is righteousness.

The Lord is awesome,

worthy of all praise;

He is the Alpha and Omega,

Beginning and End;

forever was and forever will be.

Praise the Lord for our past, present, and future.

Amen.

A RELATIONSHIP IN CHRIST

Book 1

12

Deter from solely relying on anyone,

for each person is there, when he or she wants to be.

The same goes for your friends and even

those who are in Christ.

Do not solely rely on anyone.

We are all solo in this life,

but the Lord is there always.

He knows all our thoughts,

all our needs

and all our hearts.

One can always rely on God.

He is there

in times of trouble and in poverty,

in times of happiness and joy

and in times of loneliness and uncertainty.

The Lord's love and guidance is our security.

No one can change or enhance His character,

for the Lord is Holy.

The Bible states that He is with you when you are with Him.

The Lord is present

in all places,

in all rooms

and all houses.

He is there with you on a thousand hills,

in the depths of the deepest oceans,

in the sky to the heights of the moon,

in the most remote of forests and jungles,

for He is with you when you are with Him.

Glorify God; tell the little ones that they can always rely on

the Lord.

Jesus is His name. Amen.

A RELATIONSHIP IN CHRIST

Book 1

13

In your relationship with Christ,

pray that your hearts will be humbled.

An obedient heart is like a faithful wife;

one has trust, confidence, and reassurance.

We as believers can have a relationship with Jesus through

good things and bad things,

through belief and drought,

through confidence and question,

through strength and weakness,

through hope and hopelessness, even

through reassurance and discouragement;

and through your life, He will bring you in close and reveal

Himself to you;

and Jesus will give you understanding.

Remember that the Lord is the giver of good gifts and

the problem is that we are impatient people;

we want things on our own time, not God's time.

So have patience and ask God,

"Our Father, who art in heaven with all power,"

Then Say, "God,

I would like?"

And finish by saying

"I will wait upon your powerful hands

and I will have patience

please give me?

That I may glorify your name;

Thank you, Father, for hearing me.

Amen."

The more we see God as our Father,

the more we will see His giving nature and powerful

authority.

Amen.

A RELATIONSHIP IN CHRIST

Book 1

14

The Lord will bring you to where you belong; have faith,

for this is true.

God is sovereign and in full control

of life, death, judgment, and with all matter,

for all things are done through God.

Kings are set on high as the poor are fed;

the murderer is caught as a prisoner is freed;

the widow mourns as a baby is born;

one drives a car as the other one walks;

one has the knowledge to teach as the other learns.

For the Lord is sovereign and has full control,

His power heals the addict,

stops the gambler

and fights all cravings,

so that one might give a testimony

and glorify God.

So have a relationship with the Most High.

Jesus is His name. Amen.

A RELATIONSHIP IN CHRIST

Book 1

15

Belief is like a growing tree.

A seed gives root.

It springs forward,

but it's survival depends on where it was planted.

Pray that it is not choked out by the weeds.

As the rain from heaven falls down upon the little tree, it

springs up.

Through time, your belief will grow strong and secure.

It's roots sink in deep and will be grown with principals,

morals, values and ethics.

As your belief in Christ becomes more mature,

you will develop an identity in Christ,

with dignity from Christ

and a spiritual character through Christ.

When the wind shakes the tree, it may sway side to side,

but it is forgiving

and springs back.

When it grows high, the branches stretch out;

the birds of the field perch on it.

When someone is in need for Christ,

offer that person refuge.

May God bring you all close to the Holy Bible,

for it is our foundation and our holy soil.

I pray your roots are planted in it,

for it is filled with nurturance

that the believer's soul needs to keep him or her

flourishing spiritually

and forever growing. Amen.

16

The path of life is like one of those that
is corresponding to the
mountains and the seas of the world,
for a life in sin can pull you down,
and it can drag you deep into its waters.
One may even find oneself at the bottom
of life's depths,
or even just treading and trying to keep
one's head above water.
In the end, one may even have to fight for air.
I pray to God that person does not drown.
If you are in this place in your life, pray,
pray hard.
Ask for Jesus to come into your life
that He might resuscitate you,
give you new life
and help you swim to land.

Do not reject the gospel.

Jesus died on the cross for our sins

and rose on the third day

for the gospel.

As you give your heart to Jesus,

our Lord will pick you up and bring you to level ground,

that you might die to sin and live for Him

through faith and belief Jesus will set you upon His path,

and your spiritual journey will start.

Through your prayer, He will help you keep to that path,

for it is narrow;

it leads to life.

Through time, God will bring you to His Holy Mountain,

and as you climb it, the terrain may be steep,

but it is forgiving, Praise the Lord.

In the future, you will look back

and see that you were weak but now you are strong.

It will get easier to keep up with life and to turn from sin,

for, through Jesus, sin has no hold.

With the strength we gather from Jesus, we ascend.

Along the climb, there will be ups and downs,

but it will not be like the sea,

for the climb is rewarding and secure.

Devoting your life to the Lord is hard to do when you are

in sin;

so turn from sin,

follow the Lord,

walk with the Lord,

climb with the Lord

and run with the Lord

and ascend to the top!

For the reward is eternal life. Praise the Lord! Amen!

17

The gospel came at a great cost;

it came from the shedding of innocent blood

of our one Messiah, Jesus Christ.

He is our Lord of Glory and our Blessed Redeemer,

our Holy Saviour, perfect with no flaw.

Jesus preached the gospel, and through it, we are delivered

from the punishment of our sins.

We have been justified and made alive through the life of

Christ.

His crucifixion and resurrection

were the ransom for the debt against us,

that we owed that we could not pay.

For Jesus had victory over death and Satan.

For our sins were paid for in full on the cross

not cancelled but paid for with the precious blood of Jesus

Christ.

To all How believe and have faith,

God's promises will come true through His Son Jesus

Christ.

Jesus is the fulfilment of God's word.

Each one of us has the blessing already promised.

The Holy Spirit

Jesus's work of redemption has already

been accomplished

the day He made atonement on the cross on all our behalf.

He became a propitious sacrifice who took all of humanity's sins

upon Himself and absorbed the wrath of God on to himself

outside the camp.

God bless the son of man

Our Holy king servant.

Blessed is His Holy Name.

Now, as believers, we are not condemned under the law;

We, as believers, have become saved

that we may share in eternal life.

The church has been instructed with the gospel

It is the most significant peace in our salvation, and all

scripture leads to the gospel.

Through devotion and solidarity, we are truly in the Lord's

presence.

So have love for Christ and all He stands for;

in life maintain all focused on Christ.

Don't become selfish or full of pride,

don't become spiritually divided or immoral,

don't become hardhearted and rebellious;

for the Lord came to humble us, lead us to selflessness,

establish unity and community,

heal us and deliver us from sin,

soften our hearts and bring us to obedience;

that we may be just and merciful with each other

and give full obedience to God that we will follow the Law,

the gospel, and the

Ten Commandments,

that we may turn from sin, face God, repent and be forgiven,

that non-believers might turn to the Lord and believe in

Him and put their hope

in the Lord.

I pray every man and every woman

be redeemed and saved.

Glory to the Highest; Jesus is His name.

He has come to save all humanity and deliver us from sin.

He has chosen us to be born again through the living word

of truth.

Holy Bible

(NIV®.) John 3:16 New International Version (NIV)

[16] For God so loved the world that he gave his

one and only Son,

that whoever believes in him

shall not perish but have eternal life.

In the gospel, the Lord came down from the Father,

was born to a virgin,

spread the gospel to the people;

He lived a sinless and obedient life to God.

Jesus taught many, saved many, healed many,

and fulfilled the prophecies of

the scriptures;

He came to enhance the Word but not to take away

from the Word;

He did not come to abolish the law but to fulfill the law;

to wash away all sin so that we may be blameless.

Through His resurrection, He shows us eternal life.

Holy Bible

(NIV®.) John 11:25-26 New International Version (NIV)

²⁵ Jesus said to her, "I am the resurrection and the life. The one who believes in me will live, even though they die; ²⁶ and whoever lives by believing in me will never die. Do you believe this?"

Jesus Christ is sovereign and in control of life, death,

judgment and

He knows all, sees all.

The Lord is sovereign.

The gospel means God's good news.

The message is given to all who seek it

by grace alone,

by faith alone

and through Christ alone,

that as believers we may all share in eternal life.

Amen.

A RELATIONSHIP IN CHRIST

Book 1

18

We are all called to preserve the integrity of the gospel;

do not distort it.

The truth of it must be preserved, protected, defended, and

contended

at all costs,

especially from those who are speaking heresy,

for the gospel was delivered to the saints by God,

to give us accuracy in our belief and knowledge for Christ.

That we may have great esteem for God

and that as believers we can debate against falsehood,

for there is no fast-tracking to knowing God.

The gospel is critical, for the power of God, as well as His

righteousness, is

revealed

in His gospel.

When you are in the Word, do not eclipse its meaning.

God bless; may you receive all its treasures,

for the Word tells of God's unchangeable grace and

unchangeable love,

and the teachings of Christ's doctrine;

the kingdom of heaven,

and through Christ the Word reveals how one acquires

eternal salvation.

The first importance is the gospel; it says that Jesus died on

the cross for our sins,

was buried and, on the third day, He rose.

In the gospels, God teaches us about the eternal benefit we

have as believers

and the eternal ramifications for being a non-believer.

One can compare and have contrast to make a sound

decision to have God in

one's life.

Holy BIBLE

(NIV®.) Mark 1:15 New International Version (NIV)

[15] "The time has come," he said. "The kingdom of God has

come near.

Repent and believe the good news!"

Holy Bible

(NIV®.) Mark 1:17 New International Version (NIV)

¹⁷ "Come, follow me," Jesus said, "and I will send you out
to fish for people."

So proclaim the gospel to the world,

spread the good news through this generation and the

generation to come

to all the little ones that they may have the chance to know

Christ.

We should pursue divine grace,

for this should be an essential for our future

It is through faith alone,

through grace alone,

through hope alone and through Christ alone

that we are to accept God's sovereignty

and proclaim our salvation to all who come in our path.

We are believers; we are called to know the gospel

and preach Jesus's death and resurrection.

Jesus paid for our immoral debt to God;

He paid for our penal debt as well.

Jesus died to wipe away our sin;

and He died in our place,

that He may give us eternal life.

He makes intersession for us;

He justifies us with the purity of His heart,

by His death and resurrection.

By His blood,

He made us guilt-free

and blameless; through His name we are saved;

that we may have a relationship in Christ

and not be condemned to hell

for our transgression;

That He rose from the dead,

that we will rise from the dead to be with Christ,

that He will bring us to where we belong in

the afterlife as well as in this

life,

and that we will live for eternity.

So have faith.

Receive the Lord, and by His grace, embrace the gospel,

for through the gospel, we all receive His saving grace.

First, you will acquire knowledge in your belief.

Second, you will agree that you need God and His Word,

and that His Word is true.

In both of these aspects of conversion even

the demons believe.

What sets us apart

is the third.

To have true confidence, you will truly need to

trust in the Lord,

rely on the Lord,

depend in the Lord,

put your faith in the Lord

and love the Lord with all our heart and mind.

I pray you read God's Word, learn His word,

and write it on your heart.

Seek His Word, especially the gospel. Amen.

A RELATIONSHIP IN CHRIST

Book 1

19

As the evil parts at the sides,

"it" runs through,

"it" resides in so and so, and

so and so become "it".

When one looks deep into "its" eyes,

they are empty and there is no guilt,

no remorse,

no shame,

only malice thoughts of gain.

In front, there is greed, violence, mistrust, resentment,

jealousy, and hatred.

In "its" mind are "its" evil schemes, "its" depravity,

and "its" deceitful thinking

fully takes over

the humans mind

and evil drives "it."

In "its" fullness, it is consumed within perversion

and lack of self-control, for that is "its" stem, for all "its"

madness?

"It" covers itself with pride and self-righteousness,

for "it" has no name. The Devil has made "it", and "it" is

his slave.

He has taken hold of this person and put a bridle in his or

her mouth,

and guides that person toward ill-gotten gain and falsehood.

That person has no limits; evil resides in "its" heart; it

conspires hate and

vengeance.

"It" has a selfish hunger, and "it" lives a bloodthirsty life.

At this point, "it" has no rest

and paranoia fills "its" mind

and people on every side want to take "its" life.

Those in power consumed by "it,"

know that when "it" dies, the people will cheer and

celebrate.

Even when "it" is in power, the people listened,

and walked in fear,

but when "it" dies, "it" will not be mourned.

For to the people that are in control of the streets

that enslaves one another

with addiction and prostitution,

with fear and violence.

Heed this warning; stop this kind of life, for it leads to death.

You will have to suffer the consequences for your actions,

for the Lord is sovereign. He is in control; He lives, here and right now

Everyone will have to give an account,

for He is judge; even the demons know this.

Life is but a moment in time, compared to eternity.

One will live an eternal life in heaven;

the other will live an eternal life in hell.

One thing is certain: We all live for eternity.

I pray "it" is wiped away

and "it" becomes a person, not a beast;

"it" becomes a believer, not a lost soul;

"it" becomes a brother or sister in Christ and not an enemy to God;

"it" becomes righteous and not a disgrace;

"it" becomes humble and not full of pride.

I pray "it" shows itself,

that this person may face "it"

and go to Jesus that He'd take control of "it."

Just ask God to help you,

for when I say "it," I mean the devil's hold.

Through life, Satan tries to grab hold

by filling a person with fear, doubt, and uncertainty.

He plays on our weakness;

he entices us and leads us astray to sin and destruction,

but Jesus has come to save you from the dark and bring you

into the light. Amen.

Jesus is sufficient enough,

and through Him, all things are possible,

for Jesus brings us to where we belong,

free from Satan's hold.

Have faith in Jesus. He will heal you,

and He will bring you to where He wants you to be;

have faith.

All men and women will eventually fall

at the feet of Jesus Christ.

Saved or condemned.

Holy bible

(NIV®.) Mark 16:16 New International Version (NIV)

[16] *Whoever believes and is baptized will be saved, but whoever does not believe will be condemned.*

*

So look at where you are heading; use a lamp—the Holy
Bible—
that you may share in the kingdom of heaven.
You are worth it; don't give up and don't forget that,
for strength let Jesus come into your life.
Turn from sin, He is forgiving.
The Lord will give you good guidance through the
remainder of your life.
Have faith!
Amen.

20

Brothers, sisters, I plead with you; turn your back on sin.

Repent!

For it is time to put an end to sin.

Jesus came to atone for the world's wickedness and sin

and to atone to the Most High.

Through Jesus alone, we are forgiven for our transgressions,

so make amends; be

forgiven.

Look toward the sky, and give esteem to God.

As believers, we are all His adopted children and we are a

part of His holy family,

for God is holy and pure. He is our Father, Creator, and

Author.

He has high regard for those who come in His name.

As believers, we are ambassadors of heaven.

Jesus is our awesome King; He is our Beginning and End.

Have faith to walk with Jesus;

know that He is omnipresent to all

and, through Him, death has no hold.

We should live to make Him proud.

Leave your old life behind you.

It is dead, and do not mourn for it;

leave it there in the dust.

Do not look back; move forward,

for your old life is full of uncertainty,

like a place with no doors,

just walls that reflect guilt and past sins.

Holy Bible

(NIV®.) Psalm 23:1-6 New International Version (NIV)

Psalm 23

A psalm of David.

[1] The LORD is my shepherd, I lack nothing.

[2] He makes me lie down in green pastures,

he leads me beside quiet waters,

[3] he refreshes my soul.

He guides me along the right paths

for his name's sake.

[4] Even though I walk

through the darkest valley,[a]

I will fear no evil,

for you are with me;

your rod and your staff,

they comfort me.

⁵ You prepare a table before me

in the presence of my enemies.

You anoint my head with oil;

my cup overflows.

⁶ Surely your goodness and love will follow me

all the days of my life,

and I will dwell in the house of the Lord

forever.

A RELATIONSHIP IN CHRIST

Book 1

21

The Lord has healing hands;

they watch over all;

they stretch out over the land;

they are refuge for the poor and for the needy.

The whole world is in His hands,

and when you are in need, you can always rely on the Lord.

When times of loneliness, fear, and regret wash over you,

you can always find refuge in the Lord.

I pray you find solitude

and let go of the past.

Do not stay in the past,

for the future you can change.

We all have the chance.

Leave behind all your blame,

and forgive those who trespass against you,

that you might be forgiven.

All who come in the Lord's name

may they share in the glory of God

and may they be blessed on every side.

For they will walk with the Lord, know the Lord, and share

peace with the Lord;

for the one who comes in the name of the Lord

May they be blessed with grace, prosperity,

and a beautiful family.

For you will always have Jesus in your hearts.

I pray all share in the divine relationship

that we call the gospel.

"Lord, help us not to rebel but to have strength.

I Know that I need You, for Lord

In my life I've been lost

and far from hope."

We are all familiar with the idea of a plant loving light.

It will turn and stress for light; but if one puts it in the

dark, it will shrivel up,

and if one neglects to put it back into the light,

eventually it will die.

There are many types of plants, there are some who thrive

on life and some who

thrived on

death.

Many who thrive in the light and many will parish

in the dark

We all have a choice. May the Lord find purpose for all,

that they may do His will.

The rich and the poor have two ways to go in life

the narrow path or the broad path, and we all share this in

common,

and the Lord gives sight to both.

The true detest dishonesty, and the wicked detest the true.

Now pray, pray hard.

Pray for truth;

pray for your safety from the evil one;

pray for the things you do have;

pray for the things you don't have;

pray for the little ones,

that they are far from oppression

and safe.

Pray for knowledge;

pray for wisdom;

pray for understanding.

Pray that the Lord will keep you in His light and

help you grow and thrive;

pray to the Lord that He will lead you away from falsehood

and keep you far from

temptation;

pray for your health and pray for the health of others;

pray for a closer relationship with God;

pray for strength;

pray for hope;

pray for faith;

pray for guidance.

Pray that you find true and honest love;

pray that through you, the Father's will, we'll be done;

pray that you can be more selfless and giving.

The key to a fulfilling life is just to pray.

May praying become easy to all who seek the Lord.

Because I know praying is a start to having a real

relationship with Christ.

Amen.

A RELATIONSHIP IN CHRIST

Book 1

22

Through these words, I will try to bring you to believe

and guide you to the Lord,

that you may all know and love the Lord;

that you may eat from His truth

and be satisfied

and be joined together

and be united.

Listen to His Word and feel the love that He has for each

and every one of you;

so give esteem to Him and know His love,

that when you see Him, you will recognize Him.

As a believer, you will yearn for Him and want to follow

Him;

as one walks to the beat of His drum

with full vigor, devotion and strength.

God is our Father; His motivations are developed out of

His Fatherly love and they are clear,

and they are for your greater well-being. Praise the Lord.

His thoughts are on high; He is pure through and through.

There are no words that can fully explain God

but *awesome, holy, merciful, just* and *righteous.*

It is He who gave His only Son that

we may live. Amen.

A RELATIONSHIP IN CHRIST

Book 1

23

Know the terms,

for the day of decision is here.

Read the Bible that you may know the terms.

One should have fear for God to make a sound decision

before it is too late, the fire falls from the skies, and all the

people worship the

beast;

for the people will scatter

and there will be no guidance

as one's soul will be tried and pulled to its limits;

and there will be weeping and gashing of the teeth.

Where everyone will work on impulse and there will be no

self-control

in humanity's heart.

In hell there will be no rest, no peace, and no quiet,

just sorrow, pain, and suffering.

Know that the Lord is in control and sovereign over

life, death, and judging

and

Heaven and hell.

God's wrath is to the one who denounces the Lord and to

all who embrace sin,

to all who have blood on their hands and sin in their hearts,

to all who have forgotten the Lord and followed their pride,

for that is the devil's story.

So remember we are all in the land of decision.

Choose wisely, for the time is now.

There is only two sides—light or dark,

up or down,

Heaven or hell,

Jesus or Satan,

Being a believer or a nonbeliever,

Saved or condemned;

know the terms, read the Holy Bible.

May God be with you always, and to the believer may He

be with you forever.

Amen

A RELATIONSHIP IN CHRIST

Book 1

24

These are the Ten Commandments handed down by God
to Moses:

1. Thou shall have no other god before me, and you are to
love God with all your heart, soul, strength, and mind.

2. Thou shall not make or worship any idols of any kind.

3. Thou shall not take the Lord's name in vain.

4. Thou shall honour thy Sabbath day and keep it Holy.

5. Honour thy mother and father.

6. Thou shall not murder.

7. Thou shall not commit adultery.

8. Thou shall not steal.

9. Thou shall not bear false witness against thy neighbor.

10. Thou shall not covet thy neighbor's house.

Thou shall not covet thy neighbor's wife or anything that
belongs to thy neighbor.

Holy Bible

(NIV®.) Romans 6:8-14 New International Version (NIV)

[8] Now if we died with Christ, we believe that we will also live with him. [9] For we know that since Christ was raised from the dead, he cannot die again; death no longer has mastery over him. [10] The death he died, he died to sin once for all; but the life he lives, he lives to God.

[11] In the same way, count yourselves dead to sin but alive to God in Christ Jesus. [12] Therefore do not let sin reign in your mortal body so that you obey its evil desires. [13] Do not offer any part of yourself to sin as an instrument of wickedness, but rather offer yourselves to God as those who have been brought from death to life; and offer every part of yourself to him as an instrument of righteousness. [14] For sin shall no longer be your master, because you are not under the law, but under grace.

A RELATIONSHIP IN CHRIST

Book 1

25

The good things about a family

is that it can be renewed, restored, and reconciled,

it can be brought back from the dead,

it can be brought back alive.

One needs to renew, restore, and be reconciled with God.

Accept God's covenant with you.

God seeks out our hearts; He watches over us.

God is our author.

He is the director for our lives.

In this play we call life,

we are all characters, some real and some not.

God is our creator, our author and our director. We know

our lines,

but we get sidetracked and try to rewrite the story

instead of doing God's will.

That is when one's life becomes full of sin

and far from God's plan.

So be renewed, be restored and be reconciled with God,

that your life will go well.

God is the overseer of all humanity,

a Father to all who believe in Him and all who believe in

His Son.

God is the creator of all living things;

He is the maker and creator of our living earth.

He set out all the heavens above;

they're all for His glory.

God is the "I am,"

forever was and forever will be.

He is God to all.

He is above and before all gods.

He has made a covenant through His Son for His people,

that we should all seal on our hearts.

His love is unchangeable.

God created us in His own image.

He has given us souls that will last forever.

Glorify Him by loving Him and following His

commandments.

God is awesome and powerful.

Live to glorify Him to make Him proud.

Stand in awe.

God does not take pleasure in anything evil.

With God, there is no room for wickedness to dwell in His

presence.

He is the enemy to sin and the Father to all who repent and

turn from sin.

He is pure at heart and in mind.

Just like a father, He is here to discipline and correct us.

Out of His great love for us,

He guides us that we may live,

thrive,

and grow

and not perish.

God wants to bring us close into His arms,

that we may be safe and secure from the evil one,

that we may remain in His guiding light,

that we may love Him with all our heart and mind,

that we may be His people,

His adopted children,

that we will follow His commands

and glorify Him in all we do

and make Him proud by being obedient and doing His

will.

God gave His only begotten Son

to save us from our sin.

God's love for us all, is so great that He gave His Son to die

on the cross for us,

to be a part of us, to be a part of our lives,

that He may have compassion for us and forgive us for our

sinful nature,

so through Jesus we can be renewed, restored, and

reconciled with God,

that we'd become blameless, so in turn we can come into

the presence of God.

Amen.

A RELATIONSHIP IN CHRIST

Book 1

26

Song 1

Lord I meet you in the morning,

for I wake to do Your will.

Through our relationship,

we have gained trust.

You lift me up higher and higher, until I reach the sky.

You lift me up higher and higher,

till I learn how to fly.

My love for You is getting greater and greater,

for it is a love above all.

Every day

at night I lie in my bed and pray.

The next day I awake, I'll love You the same way.

For I Praise the Lord; He lift's me up higher,

higher and higher, till I reach the sky.

He lifts me up higher and higher till I learn how to fly.

He is bringing me closer and closer

to His heart.

He brings me closer and closer;

He brings me out of the dark.

Eternal life is just around the corner.

Lord, lift me up; lift me up higher and higher,

for, Lord, I need You in my life.

God, as I lay my head at night,

I think of all things that You have done.

You have saved me through Your grace and through the

death of Your Son.

You brought me up high.

Holy, Holy, Holy is Your name.

Praise be to You. Thank You, Jesus, for You are God to all.

Awesome, Awesome is Your name.

Jesus You are the overseer of all humanity.

Thanks for lifting me up, for lifting me up higher and

higher until I reach the sky.

Lift me up higher and higher till I learn how to fly.

Higher and higher, please bring me home,

that I am with You in the heavens above.

Lord, lift me up higher;

Lord, lift me up higher.

Bring me closer;

bring me closer,

that when I die . . .

Please,

just bring me home.

Amen.

27

Song 2

Through His ultra-love,

God loves us all.

He so loved the world

that He gave His only Son

to die on the cross for our sins.

God loves us all;

He loves us all.

God loves us all;

He loves us all.

Every man, woman and child—

I pray they have a chance

to be reborn,

to die to sin and live for Christ.

To all the lost souls

Jesus offers His guiding light.

And He bestows unto you His eternal salvation and eternal
life.

So when you lay your head at night,

pray to the Highest; Jesus is His name.

For God loves us all;

He loves us all.

God loves us all;

He loves us all.

He so loved the world

that He gave His only Son to die

on the cross for our sins.

God loves us all; He loves us all.

God loves us all; He loves us all.

All men, women and children—

I pray they all have a chance

to have a relationship in Christ,

to live in community and share in unity with Christ.

We only have one life.

For our decision is to live in Christ.

Holy, Holy, Holy is His name.

All Praise goes to Christ,

for He leads us in the light;

and we yearn for Him in our life.

God loves us all;

He loves us all.

He gave His only Son

to die on the cross for our sins.

For God loves us all;

He loves us all.

For He loves us all, He loves us all.

I pray everyone has a chance;

I pray every child may be guided to Christ,

and I pray that everybody knows Him by name

For God loves us all.

He loves us all, He loves us all.

A RELATIONSHIP IN CHRIST

Book 1

28

By God giving us the Holy Spirit,

we are to listen, hear, feel, believe and act on

what the Holy Spirit is saying to us in our hearts and minds.

I pray that you may be in tune with the Holy Spirit,

for, as believers, we will be automatically credited as righteous;

as believers, we are justified by faith.

Holy Bible

(NIV®.) Galatians 3:9 New International Version (NIV)

[9] So those who rely on faith are blessed along with

Abraham, the man of faith.

The Holy Spirit is God's guiding light.

One needs to follow the Holy Spirit,

have trust in the Holy Spirit, and put one's faith in the
promise of Holy Spirit.

God's Spirit gives birth to our spirit through the living word
of Christ.

The new birth is a necessity.

The Holy Spirit continuously gives clarity and transparency
to the heart and to the mind of the saved.

The Holy Spirit speaks to God, speaks through God and
speaks for God.

The Holy Spirit knows and professes
that Jesus is our Lord and Saviour.

The Holy Spirit gives power and strength
for us to do deeds of faith
and to speak clearly to non-believers on Christ's behalf.

A believer is baptized through the Holy Spirit and
is given courage through the Father, the Son and
the Holy Spirit.

The Holy Spirit will inform you of sin in your life
and lead you back to God.

Rely on the Holy Spirit,
and by the power of the Holy Spirit working in
a person's life, Christ has pulled

that person out of the murky waters,

the Holy Spirit has given that person clarity.

We are all to pray for the Holy Spirit's help.

One cannot truly be a believer or truly repent unless the

Holy Spirit has come into

one's life and changed one's heart.

The Holy Spirit will give us drive, and it will inspire you

to do God's will.

Praise the Lord.

The Holy Spirit will help with self-control.

So ask the Lord to come into your heart

that you may be reborn and die to sin and live for Christ,

that the Holy Spirit may come into your mind, body, heart

and soul and transform

you,

that you may be humbled because your life has just changed

and your journey as a believer has just started.

The Father, the Son and the Holy Spirit;

God, Jesus and the Holy Ghost,

are one in three persons.

The Trinity will always be a part of your life as a

believer in Christ.

You will always be in God's hands.

You will always be guided by the Holy Spirit.

You will always be within Jesus's council.

Pray with an inviting heart and ask God to fill you with

the Holy Spirit. Amen.

The Holy Spirit is God's spirit,

the Holy Spirit is God's helper,

the Holy Spirit is God's source of divine intervention

working in our lives;

leading us to righteousness and holiness, helping us to

sustain obedience to God,

helping us to keep in faith, and is guiding us to live for Christ.

The Holy Spirit is like rubbing two sticks together bringing

a small ember to a big

Flame.

In our Christian lives there is much room to grow;

and the Holy Spirit spreads our flame and ignites our new

quickened, changed

and regenerated hearts

called our new birth.

Though the Holy Spirit is invisible, it is powerful,

awesome and truthful

and as believers

we put our trust in the Holy Spirit to guide us.

The believers are truly blessed, they have received the
Holy Spirit in their heart;
and the Holy Spirit's ways are always sound and true.
The Holy Spirit is gifted to everyone who receives
Jesus Christ into their
heart,
it is through God's grace that the Holy Spirit is gifted to the
believer
as a blessing.
The Holy Spirit instills truth in us and works though us for
God's glory,
for it is God's Spirit.
Through the washing and regeneration of our new rebirth
the Holy Spirit is poured out to flesh.
Through the belief in Jesus Christ and through God's grace
the Holy Spirit is our
true life source;
the Holy Spirit truly helps us keep to our walk along the
path with Christ.
God's spirit gives us confidence, patients, courage, and
strength that we will need
through our Christian walk.
We are to listen to the Holy Spirit

and allow God to speak through the Holy Spirit to us,

that the Holy Spirit will speak for us.

For the Holy Spirit is truthful and whoever loves truth,

detests the untrue.

You'll see that through truth the Holy Spirit is made

complete;

as the Holy Spirit is truth,

as God is true.

The Holy Spirit will speak to you, guide you, change you,

and restore you,

regenerate you, help you, and strengthen you.

The Holy Spirit will help us see God's love;

the Holy Spirit will help us profess God's Word to our

family, friends, and to the stranger, with confidence.

Help fight sin, provide a new life to us, cleans our darkened

heart,

help cleans our darkened thoughts,

give us a transparent vision for heavenly thoughts, desires,

and for God's will;

the Holy Spirit will awaken us.

One needs to have the Holy Spirit in them to see that Jesus

is the Lord

and to see that Jesus is God in the flesh.

So God is Jesus and Jesus is God and both of them are of

the Holy Spirit

which is God's spirit;

and which is all knowing, all seeing, all powerful, with all

authority and all

sovereignty.

The Holy Spirit helps us keep in step with God's purpose,

for the believer is being

guided by the Holy Spirit,

God's Spirit,

the Holy Ghost

Amen

Holy Bible

(NIV®.)Romans 8:1-11 New International Version (NIV)

Life Through the Spirit

8 Therefore, there is now no condemnation for those who
are in Christ Jesus, ² because through Christ Jesus the law of
the Spirit who gives life has set you free from the law of sin
and death. ³ For what the law was powerless to do because
it was weakened by the flesh, God did by sending his own
Son in the likeness of sinful flesh to be a sin offering. And so
he condemned sin in the flesh, ⁴ in order that the righteous

requirement of the law might be fully met in us, who do not live according to the flesh but according to the Spirit.

[5] Those who live according to the flesh have their minds set on what the flesh desires; but those who live in accordance with the Spirit have their minds set on what the Spirit desires. [6] The mind governed by the flesh is death, but the mind governed by the Spirit is life and peace. [7] The mind governed by the flesh is hostile to God; it does not submit to God's law, nor can it do so. [8] Those who are in the realm of the flesh cannot please God.

[9] You, however, are not in the realm of the flesh but are in the realm of the Spirit, if indeed the Spirit of God lives in you. And if anyone does not have the Spirit of Christ, they do not belong to Christ. [10] But if Christ is in you, then even though your body is subject to death because of sin, the Spirit gives life because of righteousness. [11] And if the Spirit of him who raised Jesus from the dead is living in you, he who raised Christ from the dead will also give life to your mortal bodies because of his Spirit who lives in you.

BOOK 2

A RELATIONSHIP IN CHRIST

Book 2

1

Our lives as Christians started from the foundation, which

is the faith that comes

through Jesus Christ.

It was perceived and formed from God's Word,

and it is the way our Christian house is constructed.

The Lord Jesus is our cornerstone.

He is our choice rock, which is strong and secure,

for when we are weak, through Him we are strong.

And we can find joy in the hardest of times;

for Jesus is the only way we can be saved.

Through His death and resurrection,

our salvation was bought at a great price,

for it was through the blood of Jesus Christ.

Through faith we are saved, not for our good works,

but by faith in Jesus and His death and resurrection.

The gospel—

know the gospel.

Know the terms to your salvation,

for we are to leave the world and all it has to offer behind,

and we are to pick up our crosses and walk with the Lord.

Do not look back or mourn for the days you were in slavery

to sin.

We are to die to sin and live for Jesus Christ.

The following verse is from after Jesus's resurrection when

He gave His Great Commission to His disciples.

Holy Bible

(NIV®.)Matthew 28:18-20 New International Version

(NIV)

18 Then Jesus came to them and said, "All authority in

heaven and on earth has been given to me. 19 Therefore

go and make disciples of all nations, baptizing them in

the name of the Father and of the Son and of the Holy

Spirit, 20 and teaching them to obey everything I have

commanded you. And surely I am with you always, to the

very end of the age."

As the walls of your Christian house go up,
your life will become elevated and spiritually alive within a
relationship in Christ.

Holy Bible

(NIV®) Titus 3:4-7 New International Version (NIV)

[4] But when the kindness and love of God our Savior
appeared, [5] he saved us, not because of righteous things we
had done, but because of his mercy. He saved us through
the washing of rebirth and renewal by the Holy Spirit, [6]
whom he poured out on us generously through Jesus Christ
our Savior, [7] so that, having been justified by his grace, we
might become heirs having the hope of eternal life.

For with the Lord there is much room to grow,
we will never be confined.
Fascination for God and godly things will forever expand in
our minds,

for we are always adding to our house and it should be

always growing.

It all depends on what we saturate our mind with,

for the Holy Spirit is the believers' motivation to complete

the house. I pray

that you submit to the Holy Spirit

and let the Holy Spirit drive you, let the Holy Spirit speak

to you, and let the Holy spirit speak for you.

The Lord makes our Christian life very real, through Christ

we are made alive

with attainable certainty.

Life with our Lord is never over,

and this is true, for the Lord is the epitome of love,

truth and salvation.

The Lord is

forever unraveling the mind who can perceive His thoughts

or that knows what God's will is or what His aspirations

and desires entail.

No one truly knows God just like no one truly knows you.

We can see what His powerful hand has completed

if we observe and recognize His nature in our lives;

or we may even see what is coming to completion

through revelation from the Lord;

but no one truly knows what God is doing

until it is near or at completion.

But God has given us the minds to perceive and to dream.

So if our Christian life was a house, it would have many

rooms,

many levels,

many floors,

many windows,

many doors,

many fences with many gates,

many gardens with the splendors of life.

For when the roof and the finishing touches are applied and

the believer's mind is

made up,

when one's belief is complete, through faith it will

manifested itself into reality

For it becomes a house that one can live in,

live by and live for.

The residents are you, the Father, the Son,

and the Holy Spirit.

Live in peace.

Live in relation to the Trinity.

Live in supplication with each other

and pray honestly.

Holy BIBLE

(NIV®.) Corinthians 3:16-17 New International Version

(NIV)

¹⁶ Don't you know that you yourselves are God's temple and that God's Spirit dwells in your midst? ¹⁷ If anyone destroys God's temple, God will destroy that person; for God's temple is sacred, and you together are that temple.

Love God the Father of heaven,

the God of Israel and Jacob.

One needs to love honestly and truly with one's whole

heart, mind, soul, and strength.

The Lord is the

cornerstone and foundation of our Christian salvation.

Following the Lord will show in one's life,

for the house has been built correctly,

fabricated and assembled by God's Word,

built with the tools and hand-crafted by the faith, grace and

instruction

from Jesus Christ,

developed and constructed by the stamina and

power of the Holy Spirit.

When one lives in this house, it cannot be moved or shaken,

for it is secure and well-established.

It has history.

It is not like the house that is built on the sand,

or the house that is built on a slope of mud.

Do not be like the one who relies on money

and humanistic desires or things of this world,

and do not put your heart into your possessions,

for the possessions of this world are fleeting and will decay,

but the heavenly possessions will endure forever.

Focus on the kingdom of God

and bring forth fruit.

You are to love God above all things; above your children,

your mother, your

father,

your brother, your sister and your pet and above all of

God's creations.

I tell you, do not solely rely on anyone or anything.

It only brings disappointment.

For we all have fallen short of the glory of God.

But one should rely, trust, and depend wholeheartedly

on our Lord, solely!

Give supplication to the Lord

for all your wants, all your needs, and all your desires.

You can have confidence to rely on, trust in, and depend on

the Trinity alone.

We are to rely on God for all things at all times.

Any time God gives you anything, just remember that it is

according to His riches and

glory.

Pray to God that He answers your prayers; boast about

Him to your friends, to

your family and to even the stranger when He answers

your prayers.

Boast about His forever-giving heart and

His generous hands,

for all things come from God.

That is of good nature.

For all the judges are set on high:

the throne that the King has established,

the pastors who herd their flocks,

the business owner who oversees his or her employees,

the student who learns and becomes great. Etc . . . .

Remember God has put you

there, for He has given you everything.

Do not forget Him.

Do not openly denounce the Lord

Be courage's.

Stand firm, be aware, and follow your heart,

for the Lord resides in you,

for you are His good house.

We are all temples of God.

Listen to the Lord. pay attention, for He is speaking to you.

You just need to listen.

Praise the Lord.

Amen.

A RELATIONSHIP IN CHRIST

Book 2

2

When we worship, we worship in Spirit and in truth.

As believers, we are a part of Jesus, and Jesus is a part of us.

We become one in communion with the Lord.

We are to become one and work together for the same

purpose.

Go and do your deeds of faith by faith.

Let them bleed into your lives

and, let your good deeds done through the gospel bleed

through you,

and into other people's lives.

For the work Jesus is doing in your life will become a

testament of the

faith He has given you.

For sound doctrine is married together with good works

and is acquired by Jesus's teaching of the gospel

and are good works through faith are to be for the Glory of

God.

For our deeds do not define or accredit us as being saved

and are not the grounds of our salvation.

But they do reveal God's Glory

and the grace of Jesus Christ's hand-crafted workmanship

within our lives.

If one lives by faith, good works will follow.

For no one completes something that one is proud of

and then hides it.

For our good deeds by faith should be in plain view,

for we are Christians.

Be bright and offer your light

to the one who is in the dark,

like you would help a brother or sister up from a fall,

or like you would give directions to a stranger in need

inform him or her about Jesus Christ;

and how He died on the cross and

resurrected on the third day

to bring salvation to the whole world.

And preach from the gospels—

Matthew, Mark, Luke, and John—

to your family, to your friends and to the stranger.

Help to reveal God's love for the world.

Help to reveal Jesus's message about the Kingdom of God.

Help to reveal that Jesus is God incarnate.

Help to reveal Jesus's prophetic doctrine.

Help to reveal Jesus's command for monotheism to the

people.

For the stories of Jesus are told to us to spread His message,

and the message is the good news about Jesus our Lord,

who was born to a virgin,

walked the earth, preaching, teaching, and healing,

lived a righteous, sinless, and blameless life to

God the Father.

He was crucified and died on a cross for our sins.

He was buried,

and on the third day, He rose.

Jesus walked the earth for several days;

many people saw Him.

He gave instruction to His disciples.

And then He rose to sit on His throne

to have full authority, full power and full sovereignty.

This is the gospel.

This is of utmost importance.

I pray to You, Lord, that the believers' understanding for

Your Word

becomes unlocked.

I pray to You, Lord that we all seek for Your knowledge,

and that we may grow in the Christian faith

and become secure in our belief.

And I pray that we ask for wisdom from You, Lord, that

our lives will be

safe and calm

and, when the turbulent waters arise, we

can make sound decisions

and escape the devil unharmed.

I pray for this to all who seek Your name, Lord.

I pray in the name of the Father, the Son and the Holy Spirit.

Amen

God bless all who are under the Son;

Jesus is His name.

A RELATIONSHIP IN CHRIST

Book 2

3

Our components of salvation;

first a relationship with God was broken

Holy Bible

(NIV®.)Titus 3:3-5 New International Version (NIV)

3 At one time we too were foolish, disobedient, deceived and

enslaved by all kinds of passions and pleasures. We lived in

malice and envy, being hated and hating one another. 4 But

when the kindness and love of God our Savior appeared, 5

he saved us, not because of righteous things we had done,

but because of his mercy. He saved us through the washing

of rebirth and renewal by the Holy Spirit,

Our salvation comes from Jesus

our Lord and Saviour,

with the knowledge and understanding that Jesus died for

our sins,

that He became the Lamb of salvation,

that He would save a people for His own,

that we can be saved by the grace of God,

not on our own merit, but by God's grace.

We have not earned our own salvation on our own merit,

for all our salvation comes from the

Lord Jesus Christ;

it is through His love and kindness, and by His faith He

bestows on us

we are saved.

From God's grace alone, by faith and belief in Christ alone,

we are saved

and become citizens of the Kingdom of God.

God makes us alive,

and only God can reveal Himself to us

We cannot save ourselves.

We are not capable by being saved by our own accord,

for Jesus was the ransom for our sins.

Apart from our Lord Jesus Christ, our salvation is virtually

unattainable,

I tell you, even if you are the most righteous out of Gods people.

Holy Bible

(NIV®.) Titus 3:7 New International Version (NIV)

[7] so that, having been justified by his grace, we might become heirs having the hope of eternal life.

✳

You are justified by faith in your belief for Jesus, for He is

the only way and the only

open door

to eternal life and the only way to the Father;

and I tell you, that it's not by

your good works,

for, through faith, you are given eternal life as a gift.

If you are a believer, devote yourself wholeheartedly

to the Christian faith

in the hope of being reconciled to God;

and dwell in the realm of His saving grace.

Amen.

A RELATIONSHIP IN CHRIST

Book 2

4

I tell you, live a holy life!

Turn from the secular life!

For humankind has been saved since the beginning of time.

In the Old Testament times, one was saved by faith in the

coming of Christ.

In the New Testament times, one was saved by faith in

Christ the Messiah.

In our age, we are saved by faith in Jesus Christ,

our Saviour,

and as believers we are all awaiting His return.

Talk with each other and learn from your fellowship with

each other.

Refine each other, and make disciples.

Be devoted to your prayer because prayer is the start to

having a relationship

with God.

And become devoted in your Christian worship,

for worship is essential for the believer for showing God

our gratitude and all the esteem we have for Him.

Focus on God's purpose, for we are to become selfless in

our spirit

that we may become humble and encounter God.

Please become sincere in loving God

that He may find favor in you

and reveal

Himself to you

to the point you can see Him and recognize Him

by His loving, saving and gentle hands.

Amen.

A RELATIONSHIP IN CHRIST

Book 2

5

For Jesus is the Lamb of salvation

who was sent by God

to forgive the sins of the world.

Holy Bible

(NIV®.) Proverbs 2:1-10 New International Version (NIV)

Moral Benefits of Wisdom

2 My son, if you accept my words

and store up my commands within you,

[2] turning your ear to wisdom

and applying your heart to understanding—

[3] indeed, if you call out for insight

and cry aloud for understanding,

[4] and if you look for it as for silver

and search for it as for hidden treasure,

[5] then you will understand the fear of the Lord

and find the knowledge of God.

⁶ For the Lord gives wisdom;

from his mouth come knowledge and understanding.

⁷ He holds success in store for the upright,

he is a shield to those whose walk is blameless,

⁸ for he guards the course of the just

and protects the way of his faithful ones.

⁹ Then you will understand what is right and just

and fair—every good path.

¹⁰ For wisdom will enter your heart,

and knowledge will be pleasant to your soul

Jesus is the living embodiment of God's eternal creative

principle, for Jesus

is Lord to all.

Jesus offers salvation to whoever comes to Him and believes

in Him.

We are to wholeheartedly accept Jesus honestly, and in our

hearts

with the expectation of being changed by grace.

For the gospel is written to tell us

that Jesus was (and is) God with us.

Jesus's story is told to carry a message,

and that message is the good news about Jesus

and how He came to be our personal Saviour.

Praise the Lord, for He saves all of us individually,

for individually He knows our hearts.

Amen.

Book 2

6

Holy Bible

(NIV®.) 1 Corinthians 13:2-7 New International Version (NIV)

² If I have the gift of prophecy and can fathom all mysteries and all knowledge, and if I have a faith that can move mountains, but do not have love, I am nothing. ³ If I give all I possess to the poor and give over my body to hardship that I may boast, but do not have love, I gain nothing. ⁴ Love is patient, love is kind. It does not envy, it does not boast, it is not proud. ⁵ It does not dishonor others, it is not self-seeking, it is not easily angered, it keeps no record of wrongs. ⁶ Love does not delight in evil but rejoices with the truth. ⁷ It always protects, always trusts, always hopes, always perseveres.

Holy Bible

(NIV®.) 1 Corinthians 13:13 New International Version (NIV)

[13] And now these three remain: faith, hope and love. But the greatest of these is love.

Our Lord offers love and peace of mind through salvation,

I tell you, hope is in the one who solely relies on the Lord

ask Him to save you from sin and all that it entails,

because we are helpless to do it on our own.

God Bless you.

For we are saved by faith, but we have a relationship in

Christ through

Love.

As well as knowing the Lord, we as believer are to grow in

love for Christ

for He has loved us first.

I pray that we keep close and never part. Amen.

A RELATIONSHIP IN CHRIST

Book 2

7

I tell you, God's delay is not God's denial,

for God gives to you and me;

and he also takes away

a warning to the one who seeks after the dark.

God's wrath is for the person

who willingly sins with arrogance

and thrives on evil and lives by wickedness,

who lives for and loves ill-gotten gain,

the person who has blood on their hands

and destroys and falsely convicts the innocent;

the one who leads the children of God

away and pushes them into a pit

or sets a snare for their feet,

the one who preys on the weak

and who is consumed in sexual depravity and immorality,

for this person is an enemy to the loving believer,

and to God.

There's no stopping God's burning anger to the one who

continuously sins with

no regard for obedience

or repentance.

People in this position will have to suffer the consequences

of God's wrath.

They will have to atone for their sin and be cut off.

Remember, life is given to us by God, just like food.

If you do not obey the commands and follow Jesus,

you are against God.

You're like a weed in the garden if you continuously

go against God.

When the gardener tends to the flowers,

he pulls out the weeds;

and he has no need for them, so he will throw them into

the fire.

After the Lord will stand back and admire all He has

tended, preserved, protected, and nurtured and His garden

will be complete.

Our life is very fragile,

but our strength in Christ is enduring,

for the believer, the "Christian," is of great value,

for we are far and few between,

for there are not many people who can truly say that they

love God

with all their heart, mind, strength and soul,

or honestly profess that they love Jesus as our Lord God.

Remember, God's love is great,

for He created us and, through His love, He is molding us

to be His people.

So return the love to Him by faithfully loving Him.

I pray that you become established in your Christian life.

I pray that God fills you with faith,

and I pray you share in honest, truthful and trustworthy love

for one another

and live in peace together in harmony.

Have fellowship with your brothers and sisters in Christ

to keep strong in your faith, especially for the days to come,

for they will be definitely a test to your faith,

know that the Lord is the Highest,

and I tell you, beware there's nothing hidden from the

Lord.

Jesus is His name.

A RELATIONSHIP IN CHRIST

Book 2

8

Being intimate in marriage

is to complete the home and the family.

It is to be between a man and a woman

in mutual trust

to complete the act of unity.

The two are to become a mono body.

With the hope of sharing communion together,

one should complement the other in spirit.

Both should be in relation to Christ

and mutually live to do the will of the Trinity

and with their faith linked together with the salvation that

only comes from Jesus

alone.

Sex is one aspect of the relationship,

but mutual love for one another and love for God

should be the center of the relationship's existence.

The Spirit tells us to join with a Christian,

for it is better than being alone in your faith, we are to

advance, flourish, build,

arise, breed,

mature, multiply, and thrive.

For the believer, I ask you think as one is one and two are two

for I say to you it is better to have two working together

in one faith.

Because in our faith, we know Jesus is the way to acquire

our salvation.

So initially, we want our partner to be saved with us

that our partner may partake in the generosity of faith, that

is given to us by

Jesus Christ.

We are to grow together in love and in faith

and become spiritually, emotionally and physically linked

to one another

to the point that we are one.

Holy Bible

(NIV®.) Ephesians 5:22-26 New International Version (NIV)

²² Wives, submit yourselves to your own husbands as you do to the Lord. ²³ For the husband is the head of the wife as Christ is the head of the church, his body, of which he is the Savior. ²⁴ Now as the church submits to Christ, so also wives should submit to their husbands in everything.

²⁵ Husbands, love your wives, just as Christ loved the church and gave himself up for her ²⁶ to make her holy, cleansing[her by the washing with water through the word,

So when you seek a husband or a wife,
stop and think about the Father, the Son and the Holy Spirit.
Think about if you are willing to be alone in your faith,
or are you willing to starve for Christian unity?
Or have spiritual conflict division or difference between
you and your partner?
One might even worship a different god or gods unknown.
If you love that person, can you see yourself walking down
a different path than he or she?

For there is only one way for our salvation,

and there is only one way for eternal life.

And these only come through the faith that we as believers

have

for

Jesus Christ.

Amen.

A RELATIONSHIP IN CHRIST

Book 2

9

One does not need to look back

or go to the back

when they're on their way to the front,

for whoever continues forward and does what the Lord insists

will have no need to backslide.

For the grace of God is sufficient enough to continue

walking forward,

for the reality of salvation is to the one who fears the Lord

and who is obedient and sees God's sovereignty.

It is to the one who wants to remain in the presence of

God's Glory;

I'm informing you to continue to walk tall and upright

and humble your heart,

for as believers you are heirs to God's inheritance

with the promise of eternal life.

You have treasures on earth as well as in heaven;

all you have worked for will not be lost.

Just remember what you are working for.

It is to bring Glory to God

in this life and all the way into the afterlife.

God Bless, amen.

A RELATIONSHIP IN CHRIST

Book 2

10

Holy Bible

(NIV®.) John 6:47 New International Version (NIV)

[47] Very truly I tell you, the one who believes has eternal life.

I tell you

pray without ceasing,

grow in your relationship with Jesus,

stay on the narrow path,

for it leads to life.

For your salvation is of most importance.

Set the world aside.

Your goal from start to finish

needs to be focused on Jesus,

for these are all synonymous to God.

God Bless you all.

May you find peace and tranquillity in your life,

knowing that in the end heaven is your home.

Amen.

A RELATIONSHIP IN CHRIST

Book 2

11

We are to have a malleable mind

like that of the child

instead of a stiff neck.

We need to become adaptable and tractable

by becoming soft in heart, submissive to change,

transformable in spirit,

yielding by character and nature,

become flexible in our hearts and minds and become

changed by love,

free flowing in faith,

become meek in understanding,

become obedient in fear and trembling for the Lord,

have a tame heart and spirit,

within an amendable lifestyle.

Like clay to a potter's hands,

you are to submit in obedience to God,

and by the grace of Jesus Christ become mouldable

and become new in spirit.

But in that day, you'll become stable and secure as a rock

in your belief of Jesus Christ.

The goal is to not be hard, stiff, and rigid

when you are learning about the Christian faith.

One truly needs to be like a child when following Christ.

Holy Bible

(NIV®.) Luke 18:16-17 New International Version (NIV)

[16] But Jesus called the children to him and said, "Let the
little children come to me, and do not hinder them, for
the kingdom of God belongs to such as these. [17] Truly I tell
you, anyone who will not receive the kingdom of God like
a little child will never enter it."

For when the Lord talks to you, answer Him.

For when He is pulling and tugs on your heart,

acknowledge Him.

If the Lord asks you to do something, act,

and if you are going to boast, boast in the Lord.

Boast of His death and resurrection.

Boast of His salvation

that He offers to all who believe unto Him,

for His salvation is to all colors and all walks of life.

There is no prejudice with the Lord.

Christianity is to the ones who give themselves to the Lord

as a living sacrifice.

May Peace be with you. Amen.

A RELATIONSHIP IN CHRIST

Book 2

12

The only way to receive eternal life is to receive Jesus Christ.

For the Lord's road is narrow, and the devil's road is broad

and wide;

the broad one leads to death and destruction.

The narrow road leads to eternal life and eternal salvation

one needs to make a choice

and commit.

Holy Bible

(NIV®.) John 6:47 New International Version (NIV)

⁴⁷ Very truly I tell you, the one who believes has eternal life.

*

Search out the Scripture, look to reaffirm these words

and the words of your teachers,

For our salvation does not come from the communicators

of the gospel;

but it is comes from the good message that is the gospel,

which is of great importance.

Not by the persuades of the tongue do we connect

but by the faith we have in Jesus Christ.

We are called to be loyal disciples of Christ in our Christian

faith,

and we are to become drawn into Him that we may be

formed and moulded into

Godly people,

living for and by Godly things,

aspiring to Godliness,

for we are to pick up our crosses and follow Jesus.

For one to truly be a disciple of the Lord,

one needs to fully give himself or herself to the Lord

in order for the Lord to receive you or me, we need to fully

receive Him

and submit to Him in the fullness of our lives.

We are to live by Him, live for Him, and live through Him

in our eternal walk.

We need to fight the good fight,

and through the Lord's power, we will become strong,

not weak

but disciplined, loving, faithful, peaceful, loyal, and devoted

to the Most High,

Jesus is His name.

We are to submit as disciples

to the Lord's teachings, to His guidance along the path; we

are to except His

standards of life,

fully trust in Him for all things, rely on Him in all situations,

and finally love Him in the fullness of the meaning.

For Jesus came to save us from the sins of the world.

Holy Bible

(NIV®.)John 3:16-17 New International Version (NIV)

¹⁶ For God so loved the world that he gave his one and only Son, that whoever believes in him shall not perish but have eternal life. ¹⁷ For God did not send his Son into the world to condemn the world, but to save the world through him.

The Holy Spirit has instilled in me, to tell you, to live your

life wide awake,

open-eyed,

sober-minded,

attentive,

aware,

for the evil one seeks to enslave us and deceive us

through fear, uncertainty, doubt, and evil pleasures.

Become malleable to the Holy Spirit

that you may come out of the darkness

and into the light.

By the power of the Holy Spirit

you can become changed and discard your old self.

That you may live with strength, power, and courage

that only comes from our confidence we have receive in our

salvation

that through our heart are belief and faith will become well

established

in Jesus Christ.

In this we will have a loving connection

that is

everlasting, and through hope

we will become strengthened in our

relationship with

Jesus Christ, our personal Lord and Saviour.

For His strength will be gifted to you through your belief

and your weakness will become strength through the power

of our Lord God

and the

Holy Spirit. Amen.

That you may become Godly and have the motivation to

continue in Godliness,

and Godliness is separate from bodily self-control,

which is of minute value

compared to Godliness, which is the power to sustain

patience, love, gentleness, kindness, compassion, and

empathy for one another.

For this is Godliness.

Our God is a loving, patient, just, merciful, and

compassionate God

to the fullest meaning of these words.

Become men and women of God,

disciples of the Lord Jesus Christ.

You are to be all in, not cold or lukewarm but hot

and burning with zeal for the Lord.

You are to be like soldiers walking forward in rank, not

swaying side to side

but steadfast and daily walking toward the Kingdom of

God.

So devote your life to fight the good fight

and study your Bible and stay in the Word.

Know your Holy Bible so that you can define the truth and

defend it,

for Jesus said that His sheep will know His voice,

become saturated in God's Word.

Never quench the spirit;

pursue the prize of eternal life,

daily becoming secure in your salvation,

praying for faith, praying in devotion, keeping loyal and

obedient to the Father,

continually gazing at the directions that will give God Glory.

Do not become temporal in your worship.

Do not cease from praying, rejoice always,

give thanksgiving to the Lord

for all things at all times.

Do not look back or mourn for your sinful life that you

previously had

but look forward look toward the silver lining

and run toward the prize.

The Kingdom of God, heaven, and eternal life

are at hand;

and the Lord is the one who gives it to you as a gift.

Love one another but love our God

with all your heart, soul, mind, spirit, and strength,

for this is the first commandment.

Holy Bible

(NIV®.) Matthew 10:37-40 New International Version (NIV)

[37] "Anyone who loves their father or mother more than

me is not worthy of me; anyone who loves their son or

daughter more than me is not worthy of me. [38] Whoever

does not take up their cross and follow me is not worthy

of me. [39] Whoever finds their life will lose it, and whoever

loses their life for my sake will find it.

[40] "Anyone who welcomes you welcomes me, and anyone

who welcomes me welcomes the one who sent me.

*

Your soul and your spirit are to live in sync with Christ;

as disciples we are to live through Christ.

We are to take in the fullness of the Lord,

and we are to receive Him as our personal Lord and Saviour

and grow in faith, for the end of days is coming;

it's close at hand.

He may come today,

any hour, any minute.

The Bible says that He will come like a thief in the night.

Live to see the Lord's face.

Keep clean that you can greet Him with a clean conscience.

I pray that in your Christian life you become

faithful within heart,

loyal within spirit, and devoted within mind, body, and soul

and that you may have confidence on judgment day.

For a repentant heart is like a trustworthy servant

that faces his or her master

and comes clean.

In return he or she will receive forgiveness

and will show to be a trustworthy servant;

the servant will gain courage through repentance

by his or her honesty

and love will be the result;

"trust"

instead of shame, guilt, and regret,

and in the end one's honor will be salvaged

and restored through truth.

For love is forgiving, patient, trustworthy, honest, and gentle,

for God is Love, and He shows it to us in the fullest extent

of the meaning.

One needs to love oneself before one can love others,

for this is Jesus's last Command before His death and

resurrection.

Love one another.

Amen. Bless you all.

A RELATIONSHIP IN CHRIST

Book 2

13

For Lord I submit to You,

mould me,

help me become who You will me to be,

open my eyes to understanding,

help me to think like You,

speak like You,

and act like You.

For I am lonely in body,

but You are continuously strengthening me in spirit,

for when I am weak, I am strong

that I may find joy in all times.

Dear Lord, I give You complete reverence,

for I am at the point in my faith that I know the power of

the Father, the Son, and

the Holy Spirit

is fully sustaining me.

The Trinity has completely allowed me to have clean hands

and a clean mind that is far from perversion.

The Trinity has given me bodily self-control

and the ability to become compassionate with the

weak in spirit,

loving all God's creations without prejudice,

gentle within being and grace throughout my life.

Thank You, Lord.

Finally my life is on the narrow path.

Please Lord, help me to not stumble

please give me a clean heart

that I may keep a clean conscience

and continue to seek after righteousness.

Help me to study Your Words daily

that when people come to persecute me

I may know the depths of Your gospel

and be ready.

For Jesus, I have faith in You that

You are my personal Lord and Saviour

and that You died on the cross to redeem us as sinners and

atone for the sins of

the world,

and on the third day You rose and resurrected,

and by Your resurrection we have the gift of everlasting life.

That is solely gifted by You

I Praise You Lord with all my heart for all You have done

for us

for You are the lamb of salvation,

perfect and without flaw,

sinless and blameless.

For Lord help me not to contradict You

but to share the truths about the Trinity

I pray in the name of the Father, the Son, and the Holy

Spirit.

Amen.

God Bless the seed that takes root.

A RELATIONSHIP IN CHRIST

Book 2

14

I pray to You, Heavenly Father,

fuel me with Your fruitful Words

that I may produce good fruit.

Help me to sow plentifully

that I may reap plentifully

and to have confidence

in sharing the good news

that I may make You proud God of me,

for as a believer when I came to You Lord,

You revealed Yourself to me.

I began to know You better from listening to scholars,

preachers and teachers.

I read Your Word,

and I was drawn in close.

But shame on the ones who teach

religious paranoia or hypocritical doctrine,

for they lead God's people away,

and they will have to suffer the consequences.

We are Your flock, Jesus, for we know Your voice,

for You are our Good Shepherd

and will never lead us astray.

I have faith.

Please Lord, help us to stay away from

the wolves that are in sheep's clothing,

the imposter of this age,

and the un-genuine,

the one who willingly lies to his flock

and contradicts Your Word, Lord,

but allow the gospel to be preached clearly

and transparently.

Lord, please reveal Your Word to the believer as well as the

nonbeliever

that every knee may bow

that everyone may have spiritual certainty

through faith and belief in Jesus;

and become reassured in Christ's gift of divine salvation.

Help me to testify and give a creditable testimony to

the salvation You offer Jesus to all who come to You and

receive You,

who believe and have faith in You.

Help me, Lord, to share about the great love

God the Father has for His elect,

His children.

I pray, Lord, that through Your Words

the believer becomes inspired to fulfill the will of God,

submit and become transformed by God's spirit,

and move forward in his or her vigilance in the pursuit toward

the Kingdom of God, heaven,

and that we can confirm our personal faith and

believe that we have,

in You, Jesus Christ daily.

For our Heavenly Father is God to all,

believer and nonbeliever,

righteous and unrighteous,

holy and unholy,

for our Heavenly Father is God to all,

and He listens to whoever prays to Him

with a humble heart.

Amen.

A RELATIONSHIP IN CHRIST

Book 2

15

Do not seek to destroy one's temple with hate

or invoke lawlessness

but instead fight to salvage one's temple

with love and kindness.

Even if one pays you with evil,

repay that person with

the goodness of your heart

that you may heap coals on thier head

and have hope in that person that he or she may see the

goodness of God in you

and see his or her fault

and turn from his or her evil ways

and come to Christ.

Show mercy to the weak in heart

and pray for the one who is faint in spirit

and to the one who has no shepherd to follow,

for that person is lost and far from God.

For we were all once weak and blind and far from God

and separated from His presence;

some more than others.

For sin has over taken each of our lives

in some way or another,

Satan has tempted us, deceived us, taunted us,

and trapped us,

and in these times it feels

that no matter what we do or how hard we try, we seem to

get entangled in sin,

and when we run from sin, eventually sin captures us,

for that is why we need Jesus to help us fight sin

and help us to turn away from sin in our lives.

For I tell you the only way is to

fully rely on the Lord in all times,

fully depend on the Lord for all your needs and to answer

your prayers,

have faith,

believe.

We are to fully trust in the Lord completely,

and trust the Lord that He will honestly defend you,

preserve you,

nurture you, and protect you.

For in our success we need to see that the Lord promotes

goodness in our lives.

The Lord prevents anything from coming in the way of our

goodness.

The Lord provides us with the tools we need to

prosper in life.

The Lord gives us grace to perform His will through us.

The Lord tends to us to help us grow.

The Lord counsels us with the intent that we will succeed.

The Lord protects us from the evil one and leads us away

from all his deception,

for the Lord wants to see you succeed

that by our success we will glorify God the creator

and give thanksgiving

to Him for all He has done

for our past, present, and future.

For the enemy to God is Satan, but through Jesus he has no

hold over you,

even in death.

The believer is God's child,

and we are protected.

But apart from the Lord's saving grace,

I tell you that you are helpless to save yourself,

and in sin we are separated from God

through division.

For God is holy and pure,

for one does not put mud into a clean glass of water

then drinks it,

do they?

No!

But puts pure into pure

clean into clean

and dirty into dirty,

for before we are changed by the Holy Spirit,

our minds and our hearts are initially full of perversion.

Holy Bible

(NIV®.) Genesis 6:5-6 New International Version (NIV)

⁵ The Lord saw how great the wickedness of the human race had become on the earth, and that every inclination of the thoughts of the human heart was only evil all the time. ⁶ The Lord regretted that he had made human beings on the earth, and his heart was deeply troubled.

✳

For we are continuously after worldly pleasures,

but the Lord alone has the power to clean our hearts and

minds of evil and

wickedness,

for He will wash the stains from our sins, white as snow.

He give us new birth

He takes out our hearts of stone and gives us new hearts of

flesh.

that are made alive and heaven bound.

regenerate our spirit,

forgive all our sins,

replenish our dignity,

strengthen our character,

salvage our identity,

offer us His grace which is awesome and powerful,

relieve us from sin,

save us from death and destruction,

and open our eyes to the Kingdom of God, heaven,

that we may partake in eternal life

may our Glorious Father

reveal His plan to you for the days to come.

Amen

A RELATIONSHIP IN CHRIST

Book 2

16

As the light pores into the believer,
the Lord bestows His grace upon the believer.
God's Grace is not earned His grace is given
"Graciously."
We all have broken God's laws, but though God's great
mercy and love
He has offered us the forgiveness for our sins
and pardons us as law breaker's
through His son, Jesus Christ.
The faith and belief Jesus Christ enables us with
accredits us as righteous through Jesus's righteousness.
Grace is the undeserving forgiveness of our sins,
Grace is the undeserving gifts that God gives us,
Grace is the undeserving mercy God gives us,
and grace is the undeserving kindness God gives us.
"Dear Lord I pray your grace remain upon us."
God's grace enables
the believer's life to be conformed to Christ,

the regeneration of our new birth is given to us by God's
word and His grace.

Grace is given to empower our devotion and obedience to
God.

"Be a grateful servant"

God's grace alone is sufficient enough for our lives,
by God's grace we remain in His love.

It is the followers decree to living a life within a
relationship in Christ

but only by God's grace alone can we remain in Christ.

The Lord's salvation is only through the power of God's
redeeming quality
of saving grace.

As believers we are being fully sustained by the power of
the Holy Spirit,
by grace alone, through faith alone
in Christ alone.

We are to be fully reliant on His grace.

We need to have our relationship be evolved and saturated
in God's word,
for heavenly grace is a gift,
and one will never really know its importance until it's gone
or absent from one's life.

For through grace ones heart is truly made complete for
good works and to carry out the

divine will of God.

For God's grace is given to enable us to bring glory to God,

and to give us the ability to sow and to spread the gospel,

for grace is everything to the believer.

It is the undeserving love and mercy God has for sinners

that take up refuge in His Son.

Without grace we would all be wiped off the face of the

plant

Because we are all sinners and without God's forgiveness

and grace we would

All be condemned to hell and death.

and in turn without God's grace life would be separate from

God's blessings

which is grace.

Without grace, there would only be God's wrath

because we

have all fallen short of the glory of God.

and are deserving of a just judgment

we would only have a just God

not a gracious and merciful God

but our God is just, merciful, and gracious as one.

He is merciful on those he is merciful to and just to those

who he is just to

So grace is everything to the believer.

To have God give you a graceful way of life is to live with
integrity,
with having one's life refined and balanced through
devotion and obedience to God in a place where worship is
the heights of your life;
Being sanctified by Christ and edified by
His church.
It is though Christ; we obtain access by faith into this grace
in which we stand.
Our need for grace should be at the height of our prayers,
for grace allows us to,
to fight the good fight by grace we preserver.
keeping Christ at the center of all we do in our lives,
that we will focus on Him
through God's grace alone.
As God's children
We are not under law but under grace.
So pray that the Lord keeps giving you His grace
in all times, in all places.
By the grace of God,
pray without ceasing
for the Lord's unchanging, awesome, amazing
grace.
Amen.

Book 2

17

It has been our motive since the beginning of time to do it

our way,

not God's way,

but in turn we have all fallen short of the glory of God.

Holy Bible

(NIV®.) Judges 21:25 New International Version (NIV)

²⁵ In those days Israel had no king; everyone did as they saw

fit.

For Jesus's ministry on earth

was engaging, compelling, and magnetic,

for Jesus spoke with authority.

He was merciful,

He forgave sin,

healed the ill,

fed the hungry,

casted out demons,

gave sight to the blind,

helped the cripple walk

"preached and taught"

about the Kingdom of God,

He called us all to repentance that we may be reconciled to

the Father,

and when He asks us to forsake our way

and adopt His way,

people turned cold, became separated, and for some, His

way became too much,

and the result is that there became division.

It is best said in . . . .

Holy Bible

(NIV®.) Matthew 10:34-39 New International Version (NIV)

[34] "Do not suppose that I have come to bring peace to the

earth. I did not come to bring peace, but a sword. [35] For I

have come to turn

"'a man against his father,

a daughter against her mother,

a daughter-in-law against her mother-in-law—
36 a man's enemies will be the members of his own household.'[

37 "Anyone who loves their father or mother more than me is not worthy of me; anyone who loves their son or daughter more than me is not worthy of me. 38 Whoever does not take up their cross and follow me is not worthy of me. 39 Whoever finds their life will lose it, and whoever loses their life for my sake will find it

✳

Apart from the Lord enabling us, regenerating us, and revealing Himself to us,
we will never know Him and will not come to Him
and will be separated from being reconciled to
God the Father.

Holy Bible

(NIV®.) Matthew 10:40 New International Version (NIV)
40 "Anyone who welcomes you welcomes me, and anyone who welcomes me welcomes the one who sent me.

✳

Holy Bible

(NIV®.) John 6:40 New International Version (NIV)

[40] For my Father's will is that everyone who looks to the Son and believes in him shall have eternal life, and I will raise them up at the last day."

So acknowledge who Jesus is
and embrace the Lord,
for He is our source of hope and our only source of
everlasting life.
Be convinced,
for the selfishness of humankind has been the motive
for us to do it the "world's way,"
not God's way.
For Jesus meditated and prayed daily through
His whole mission
with the full intent
that we would forsake our way and adopt His way.
For this makes sense when you see that
apart from the Lord enabling us to believe and gifting His
faith to us,

we are alone and disconnected from being enlightened

through truth,

and we are detached from being regenerated through God's

grace and

have the power of the Holy Spirit dwell in us.

Apart from the Lord Jesus Christ's love,

we will not come to the Lord, for apart from His work in

our lives we

will never forsake our way

and die to sin and live for Jesus Christ.

Unless we adopt His way, we are on a deadly course to

inevitable

destruction.

So listen to the Lord.

He communicates logic,

He communicates truth,

and He communicates love

in a compelling way.

He communicates through revelation,

He communicates through divine intervention,

He communicates though visions,

He communicates through dreams,

He communicates through God's Word in the Holy Bible,

He communicates through all powerful prayer,

He communicates through the mind, the heart, the spirit,

and the soul,

and the Lord shares with you

His knowledge, His wisdom, and His understanding.

Apart from divine grace, one cannot acknowledge Jesus as

the Son of God

and as our Lord and saviour,

for when you are with the Lord, the Lord is with you.

When you seek the Lord, He will be found by you,

and He will be there with open arms.

Receive Him that He will receive you.

Ask that He reveal Himself to you

that you may have a revelation

and become

secure in your belief.

Knock that your heart will be opened

to the regeneration that only comes from the power of the

Holy Spirit.

Ask that you will be part of the Father's will, and you shall

receive,

for we need God's grace working throughout our lives

and paired together with His illuminating light

that we may share in the fullness of the spirit of Jesus Christ,

for if our spiritual life is not completely rooted in Christ,

then we have no life.

Do not be fooled with anything else.

The Lord is the giver of life,

the taker of life,

the one who gifts eternal life,

the one who judges and forgives sin,

and He has the power to condemn us.

For if you are not in Jesus Christ,

according to Scripture, you are not saved

but dead in your sins.

In that state you are separated from God and His grace,

and when you die, you will die in your sins,

and, as Jesus says, the only place that will be waiting for this

person is filled with

weeping and gashing of teeth,

for I tell you, do not reject Christ in your life.

The only way for your eyes to become open and believe

is to have God reveal Himself to you

to become introduced to Christ through the gospel

and to be transformed, changed, and regenerated

by the very person of the Holy Spirit.

And only through our new understanding, our new

quickened change,

and our new righteous conversion

will we ever know or come to Christ,

for every man and every woman on the planet

needs divine assistance, and apart from Jesus,

one is dead in spirit.

So I tell you truly, put all your confidence in the Lord alone.

Jesus is His name, Amen.

May God's grace be with you.

A RELATIONSHIP IN CHRIST

Book 2

18

This day and age the world's thoughts, desires, and motives
are focused on the pleasures of self-hungers, cravings, lust,
and idols.
We have an appetite for worldly wants,
not needs or necessities,
for we are at the point in this world that
our wants have become needs, everything we want we have
convinced ourselves we need. In addition, covetousness has
become a way of live;
from baby to old age we want what other have and are
ungrateful for what we do have this is a grave sin.
To be ungrateful and desire in your heart something
another person has is covetousness
Jesus says, "beware of covetousness" several times in scripture
probably because it is something we all forget is a sin
when we should be counting our blessing that the Lord has
given us our

necessities, and needs.

It is just like a child who has a sample of chocolate ice

cream,

then one of caramel,

and one of vanilla ice cream,

one after another.

In the end, he or she is left with an empty plate,

unsatisfied,

still wanting more,

for we do not bring to account what the Lord has given us

but focus on what we do not have.

In the human heart there is never enough,

and there is no amount that will appease

or quench our list of desires,

for we can easily come up with a list of them on a whim,

for if our wants, need, and desires are continuous,

then we need to know that God the Father is the giver of

good things,

including good spiritual gifts.

And the Lord says that He will give us our needs; all you

have to do is ask,

and you shall receive.

So before you ask, think.

What is it that you are asking for?

Is it a heavenly or worldly want or need,

a Godly gift or an evil pleasure,

a selfless need or a selfish want?

For in the end one leads to spiritual fulfilment, true

gratification,

and peace of mind.

The other leads to dissatisfaction, regret, and misfortune,

and God is pure and holy.

He only gives good gifts.

It is our impatience that gets in the way

from being truly

blessed.

The key when making a decision is to Glorify God

and think before you ask

about your motive,

for we as believers need to be equipped,

for Jesus brought the gospel, and we preach the gospel.

For the world in this day and age preaches and promotes

sex, lust, money, and image.

So I say examine the desires that are in your heart, in your

mind, and in your soul

and come to God with a humble heart

and ask!

God Bless.

A RELATIONSHIP IN CHRIST

Book 2

19

Do not give with the precepts

that your future will just rain away,

but be a cheerful giver

with the intent to help the gospel and further God's Kingdom,

whether it is to feed a hungry mouth

or to fund a leader, teacher, or preacher

of the gospel

or even to provide the heating, lighting, or mortgage

of the church;

they are all to promote the gospel.

Give in faith that your tidings will be blessed

and that they will become a tool for a Godly purpose.

When you give, remember that God the Father is the giver

and the provider of all your needs.

So in turn God has given you everything

that you may have the chance to give back

and give to His cause,

and through His generosity you may be generous,

and through the Lord providing to your house,

you will provide to His house

and further the gospel and the fame of Jesus Christ.

Holy Bible

(NIV®.) 2 Corinthians 9:6-7 New International Version

(NIV)

Generosity Encouraged

⁶ Remember this: Whoever sows sparingly will also reap

sparingly, and whoever sows generously will also reap

generously. ⁷ Each of you should give what you have

decided in your heart to give, not reluctantly or under

compulsion, for God loves a cheerful giver.

✳

So do not think

that if you give, your future will somehow wash away

or rain away.

Please do not think your giving will

take away from your prosperity,

for it will add to it, be good stewards.

For I tell you that the furthering of the gospel

is of most importance,

and the believer is the fuel

that ignites the engine,

and we all have faith as the Lord drives us into the future.

God Bless.

May love be in your heart.

Amen.

20

Parable

The two get ready for the race.

One has prepared themselves,

the other has not.

As they are getting ready,

the coach tells them to drink plenty of water

and to stay hydrated throughout the race.

He tells them this because it is a long race.

In the end the coach relies on them to be ready.

When the race starts the two took off fast,

but only one drank the water,

and only one had prepared themselves.

And after time goes by,

the one who did not drink water and did no preparation

tired and gave up

due to exhaustion.

But the one who had drank the water and became fully

hydrated

and prepared days and weeks and years in advance

did not give up

and completed the race.

For he or she won the prize

for the water is the Holy Spirit.

"Drink,"

and through God's Word we become hydrated.

"Drink,"

and through Jesus we gain the will and drive to complete

the race.

And He gives us guidance through our preparation,

and the prize is eternal life.

I tell you it is the Father's will

to see you succeed

and make it home.

Amen.

BOOK 3

A RELATIONSHIP IN CHRIST

Book 3

1

The mysteriousness of God's plans boggles the mind.

Lord, You alone have rescued the believer from

the devil himself.

Through Your grace, Lord, You have brought us

to a place in life

where we can be safe from the devil's clutches and from the

evil within ourselves.

Through Your grace, Lord, may we be safe to

openly profess Your name to the

people.

Oh Lord, please watch over us, protect us, deliver us

and have compassion for us,

for Your Spirit is within us.

As believers, we have the Holy Ghost;

and as we see God's providence we are revealed the nurture

of the Holy Spirit, our lives are being preserved by the Holy

Spirit,

and protect through power Holy Spirit with in us.

we initially become grateful that we are led by You, Jesus;

and my hope is that life may go well.

My old life was like a violent storm.

The hard rain and flashing lighting had swept over the

ground, my foundation;

and it had devastated the land.

It's destruction was visible to the naked eye;

my family and my friends

did not recognize me.

I was consumed by addiction and sin,

and through God's discipline,

I was under His wrath, for it was upon me.

There was nowhere to run; the walls were falling down

around me.

Humanity, which is under God's wrath,

can have only two outcomes:

one, you will become hard-hearted and hide from God,

or number two, you will accept Jesus Christ and

become drawn in

and become closer to Him.

You must understand that when you are reconciled to God,

your heart

will be at peace.

God's wrath and His discipline are to make you

come closer to Him;

and that you may be re-corrected and desire to repent for

your sin,

that Jesus can save you from your sin

by giving you strength to fight sin.

The Lord was on this earth, and He walked a blameless life,

so that

whoever comes in His name and is baptized through His

name will be justified,

and, in turn, that person will be blameless and pardoned

and his or her sin will be forgiven.

When you are in sin,

you initially have no understanding of Christianity,

you will have low self-control,

low knowledge of life and the after death,

you are in need of much truth for living your present life.

Without sound doctrine, you are filled with perversion of

mind, body and soul,

you might have an addictive mindset where slick (Satan) is

in control,

you may have weak morals, values and ethics, and they may be in need of repair.

A person living in sin will be low in wisdom which is only acquired by the Holy Bible.

Sound wisdom is what you will need to fulfill the rest of your life safely.

When living in sin, you will be lacking in faith and may not even have the

means to acquiring it; this makes for a bleak walk through life.

You may be filled with guilt and regret for not being forgiven of

your sins or spiritually unresolved offences.

When you commit a sin, you are dead in your transgressions, you are dead in sin, dead to your self-character,

you'll have a disconnected identity

and you can even be erratically depraved; and a shattered nature maybe the

result of sin.

A person in sin trespasses against the Lord, and all He stands for.

This person may even denounce Jesus as Lord, the Lord of themselves, the Lord of the world, or the Lord who is over all flesh,

but as scripture says He is Lord over all lords, and King over
all kings;

for Jesus is sovereign and possesses supreme authority.

He is the Highest.

He alone has independent authority.

Christ is dominant over Satan and his power,

and He is in control permanently.

He is to be raised to Heavenly Glory.

We are to put Him in a bright light in our lives that He
may light up brilliantly

across the whole earth that every man and women on this
earth may know Christ

and exalt Him as the Highest.

We are to give glory to God as in worship,

for He is deserving of all worship,

for He is praiseworthy.

I look at Him with awe, for He is magnificent.

He is Holy Bliss.

Knowing God and loving Him truly with all your heart and
mind is you're highest

height for prosperity, and it will be your greatest
achievement yet.

Glory, Glory, Glory to the Most High

Jesus is His name.

A RELATIONSHIP IN CHRIST

Book 3

2

When I was living in sin,

I was a wretch.

I was a miserable and unhappy person.

My way of life was despicable.

I lived a vile and a sinful life.

I lived a poor quality of life, with no real ability to navigate

or have any structure within my life.

Basically, I lived with an "if it feels good, do it" attitude for

my life,

totally unaware of the consequences and the ramifications

of the decision

I had made for my life.

When I look back, I call this being blind.

As soon as I came to the Lord and started to read from the

Holy Bible, God spoke to me

through His truth.

His truth leapt off the pages,

and I was hooked on His Word.

Like food to a starving mouth

or like a baby to a bottle, I couldn't get enough.

The Word of God took hold of my heart, and it led me to

the truth, through Jesus.

I was pulled out of the murky waters.

I could see and I could see clearly.

I got an overview and a transparent look at the past, present

and future

direction of my life.

All the lies others told me and all the lies I told myself

were visually apparent, for I had been rescued.

As the Holy Spirit entered me,

my sins and offences against God became obvious,

and it was certain that I had to change my life,

and it was apparent that, through Jesus, my

salvation, my deliverance, my emancipation and my

redemption

came solely from the belief of

the Father, the Son and the Holy Spirit.

May God Bless all who seek out the Lord

and embrace His truth.

God Bless the person who loves honesty,

for he or she is a friend to long life.

All who believe will reside in the safety of God forever.

When I gave my heart to Jesus,

I say to you honestly from the bottom of my heart,

everything changed.

At that point, I knew that the devil had no hold in my life,

and I was totally free to speak to God through prayer and

through His Word,

the Holy Bible.

His Word extremely changed my life forever.

Of the things that I have read in the Holy Bible,

some have already come to pass in my life.

For the Lord's promises to you will come true,

have faith. Here is one of my favourite Bible verses:

Holy Bible

(NIV®.) Ephesians 6:10-20 New International Version

(NIV)

The Armor of God

10 Finally, be strong in the Lord and in his mighty power.

11 Put on the full armor of God, so that you can take your

stand against the devil's schemes. 12 For our struggle is

not against flesh and blood, but against the rulers, against the authorities, against the powers of this dark world and against the spiritual forces of evil in the heavenly realms. 13 Therefore put on the full armor of God, so that when the day of evil comes, you may be able to stand your ground, and after you have done everything, to stand. 14 Stand firm then, with the belt of truth buckled around your waist, with the breastplate of righteousness in place, 15 and with your feet fitted with the readiness that comes from the gospel of peace. 16 In addition to all this, take up the shield of faith, with which you can extinguish all the flaming arrows of the evil one. 17 Take the helmet of salvation and the sword of the Spirit, which is the word of God.

18 And pray in the Spirit on all occasions with all kinds of prayers and requests. With this in mind, be alert and always keep on praying for all the Lord's people. 19 Pray also for me, that whenever I speak, words may be given me so that I will fearlessly make known the mystery of the gospel, 20 for which I am an ambassador in chains. Pray that I may declare it fearlessly, as I should.

Holy Bible

(NIV®.)1 Thessalonians 5:16-19 New International Version (NIV)

[16] Rejoice always, [17] pray continually, [18] give thanks in all circumstances; for this is God's will for you in Christ Jesus. [19] Do not quench the Spirit

A RELATIONSHIP IN CHRIST

Book 3

3

Song 3

Lord, You watch over me.

For You are in my heart,

there's no pulling us, no pulling us apart.

You lead me far, far away from the dark, far away from sin,

for I am with You

in heart and mind,

for I am with You,

I am with you, Lord, I am with you.

Lord, I am with You,

within my heart and mind.

You watch over me, day and night.

Days will come and days will go,

but one thing is certain: We are one mind, body and soul.

The Holy Spirit is guiding me,

for I have accepted the Lord's authority.

The Lord loves us; this I know is for sure,

for I stay alive through the Lord alone.

I stay alive through Him.

For I stay alive through Him.

I stay alive through the Lord alone,

for He alone leads my life.

He alone, leads my life.

For He alone, leads my life.

He alone leads my life.

Praise the Lord for His name is Holy.

He is Holy through and through.

Holy, Holy, Holy.

The Lord let me in; He let me into His life

that I may worship His name to the heavens above!

The Lord let me in,

for He let me into His life.

He let me in

that I may share in the truth of the gospel.

And the Lord fights to relieve me from all my sin.

Thank You, Lord, for letting me into Your heart,

for letting me into Your life

that I may sing Your name to the heavens above!

Thank You, Lord, for letting me in,

for letting me into Your life

that I may be changed

and have the chance to be reborn.

Lord, I love You with all of my heart,

as I worship to the heavens above.

You are Holy, You are Holy,

for You are Holy

till the end of time.

You are Holy

till the end of time.

A RELATIONSHIP IN CHRIST

Book 3

4

When I preach to you, I am trying to inform your mind

and stir your heart

so that I may charge it to action,

so that what I say to you will be used as action for your life,

for through faith the Lord gives us strength.

The Lord imprints His faith upon us with the

purpose of constructing a

relationship with us that is secure,

and with faith, He elevates us so we have power

throughout our lives;

for through time, our relationship in Christ will become

securely established and

unshakable.

The Lord's desire is that the faith that He gives you

will manifest itself into reality

within your Christian life.

The most important reason for preaching is to glorify God;

so I pray that I may be in tune with the Holy Spirit

and that I am not contradicting to God's teachings,

for I have acquired the cognizance from the Holy Spirit

and I am well aware that I need God's divine assistance

to preach to you.

And I am very thankful that God is committed to

all His people,

that He takes the time to reveal Himself to us.

We cannot know God without Him revealing Himself

to all His people,

as we are isolated from Him by our sins.

And the only way you can know Jesus is if He reveals

Himself to you.

Christianity is a belief that is revealed,

not just learned overnight.

It will take a lifetime and an eternity in heaven to get a

glimpse of God

and all He has done, for His glory is

Everlasting to Everlasting.

Christ needs to disclose Himself, that He will be revealed

through revelation to you,

you will see that He is the Lord, the Son of God.

Only the Lord can unlock our understanding.

Jesus teaches us about the sovereignty of God.

In the beginning we are all blind, desperate, broken and

living in sin.

Jesus is the Lord; He came down to earth to be in flesh,

for Jesus is God incarnate

Many people have denounced Him,

but blessed are those who embrace Him

and give their heart to Him.

Jesus is Lord to all.

There are no disappointments in sharing your heart with God

Praise the Lord. Amen.

Give Him all your trust,

for He is Everlasting to Everlasting.

A RELATIONSHIP IN CHRIST

Book 3

5

God draws us close into Himself,

through His son Jesus Christ.

Fulfilling the law in obedience is our human standard,

but fulfilling the law is impossible and initially

unattainable.

We all fall short of the law.

Through Christ's name, we are credited as righteous.

Through His grace, His name and His crucifixion and

resurrection,

we can be justified for our sins.

Through belief in the Lord Jesus and the gospel, we are saved,

for I forgive myself and God forgives me too,

for we need God, for God takes divine measures to instill

His light in us,

for we are saved by the blood of Jesus.

No one can or will believe in God unless God works in

one's life.

So ask God to reveal Himself to you; seek Him out, for the

reward is great.

And pray to God to introduce you to His Son Jesus.

I pray to God that He reveals His truth to you

and that you write His Words onto your hearts.

I pray that you may understand His Words and the Words

He has given,

that they have been sent to you by the power

of the Holy Spirit.

I pray you have a revelation from God about the

importance of the words

in this book,

and in the most important book for all humanity's greater

well-being,

the Holy Bible, which all my credit goes to,

and that you put all of these Words into action in your life;

that you share God's Word with your family and introduce all

you know to the Holy Bible;

that you read it to your children and offer them divine

guidance that is from the

gospel, for it is for our greater well-being;

that you all may be taught by Jesus and come to Him.

Seek Jesus out,

receive His grace,

be saved and be justified.

Through repentance

and by faith, be forgiven for your sins;

and be reconciled and have closure in your relationship

with Christ;

that you will become an adopted child of God, and that He

will be your Father;

and you will be His son or daughter.

And on earth, you are to follow Jesus along the path He has

given you,

because it is tallied for you.

You, as a believer, are an ambassador to heaven

that in the end of your life you will know where to go, to be

face-to-face with

Jesus Christ.

Jesus says that He will bring us to where we belong,

so as Christians, we have faith and believe in Jesus,

and as believers, in our hearts, we know that He will never

desert us.

We will die and be resurrected in spirit.

One will go to heaven, and the other will go to hell,

and both will live for eternity,

within heaven or hell.

But in heaven,

the believer will

rise to be home and be welcomed at the gates of heaven

for eternity,

and he or she will sing Praises and Worship to God.

All who enter heaven will glorify the Lord with tears of joy,

for finally they will meet face-to-face.

Jesus will be glorified for all that He has done in our

Christian lives,

and we will all worship Him and give Him recognition,

for, God Bless, He has never abandoned us or left us behind.

As you look back over your life in your older years, you will

see what you

have done.

Some will have many regrets, some will reflect against their

wicked lives of sin.

They either repent or turn their back on God,

and some will cry tears of joy, knowing that

they followed God

and that they are at the right place in their lives where God

wants them to be.

God has reassured all the old and the young alike

that He lives.

We, as believers, will hopefully see that God was, is and

always will be there along

our path.

Whether walking with us or carrying us, God is always there.

And the Lord is always there watching over us.

For He is omnipresent,

He is present in all places at all times.

Remember, God is pure and without flaw; we are the ones

who veered off His

path.

What stops us from having peace is our disobedience and

our endless

offences

against God.

To grow we need to live in obedience by

committing deeds of faith for God.

We truly need to commit to the Lord, and by His Saving

Grace alone, we can

start

to turn from our sin.

And when you commit a sin, name that sin and repent your

sins to the Lord.

So when it comes to you again, you can recognize it

and turn your back on it.

Finally, ask the Lord to forgive you, that you may be forgiven.

Like a good father to a child,

just image a child who has gone and done something

against his or her father,

and the child knows that he or she has done an offence to

the father.

If the child is not comforted, he or she will cry and cry, for

he or she knows

their offence.

The child will wait for the father to let him or her

know it's all right

and that he forgives the child;

the father is the only one who can relieve the

child's feeling of guilt.

But if the father says nothing and the child does not say sorry,

there can be no forgiveness, but there will be friction

between them

and the child will cry and cry

because he or she will not have closure. Their relationship

will be unrestored,

and the only thing blocking peace

is the period until the child repents.

When the child says sorry and the father accepts the

apology, then the child will go

off and continue playing and hopefully learn from the

mistake.

So just imagine all your sins and offences that have not

been forgiven in your life,

and there was no repentance, and that we have not said

sorry for,

I tell you this that is how one becomes dead in sin

or dead in one's transgressions.

This is when one truly needs Jesus to intervene,

and to help turn God's wrath away.

I pray deep in my heart that we all accept the Lord's teachings,

His sovereignty and authority.

May it play over in your heads that the Lord is sovereign

and in full control

of life, death, judgment and all matter.

He has full authority over the whole earth,

whatever is on it and in it and over all flesh.

The Lord has authority over

the heavens above and all the angels and the citizens in heaven;

The Lord has authority over hell, all the demons and the

devil himself.

There is no stopping Him or holding Him back,

for He has infinite power and might.

Be forgiven and be reconciled with the Father, the Son and

the Holy Spirit. Amen.

A RELATIONSHIP IN CHRIST

Book 3

6

Holy Bible

(NIV®.) John 6:41-51 New International Version (NIV)

41 At this the Jews there began to grumble about him because he said, "I am the bread that came down from heaven." 42 They said, "Is this not Jesus, the son of Joseph, whose father and mother we know? How can he now say, 'I came down from heaven'?"

43 "Stop grumbling among yourselves," Jesus answered. 44 "No one can come to me unless the Father who sent me draws them, and I will raise them up at the last day. 45 It is written in the Prophets: 'They will all be taught by God.'[a] Everyone who has heard the Father and learned from him comes to me. 46 No one has seen the Father except the one who is from God; only he has seen the Father. 47 Very truly I tell you, the one who believes has eternal life. 48 I am the bread of life. 49 Your ancestors ate the manna in the wilderness, yet they died. 50 But here is the bread that

comes down from heaven, which anyone may eat and not

die. 51 I am the living bread that came down from heaven.

Whoever eats this bread will live forever. This bread is my

flesh, which I will give for the life of the world."

*

Ask the Lord to share His illuminating light with you,

that He may give you the ability to know Him.

I have hope that Jesus will give you the desire to hear His

powerful words

and reveals true understanding to you.

As non-believers, new believers, and mature believers, we

need the Holy Spirit

to attend within us throughout our heart, mind, soul and spirit,

that we may accept what God is truly saying to us,

that we may know true love and it may be complete within

our lives.

I pray that the Lord unlocks our understanding

and opens our hearts, opens our eyes, opens our ears, and

opens our minds.

And in turn I pray that we may accept God's ministry in

our lives,

for the Lord alone liberates our spirits to speak His word to

our families and

friends and to the strangers whom we come in contact with.

The Lord alone liberates our spirit to hear, to listen,

to learn and to acknowledge God's Word,

that we my gain confidence within our Christian belief and

stand firm on

judgment day.

As I have already said, Christianity is a revealed religion.

We, as believers, have not learned about Christianity by the

academic process.

Even though we need academics for learning about it,

there is no fast track to know and love God with all our

heart and mind.

We truly need God to reveal His divine nature to us,

so that it becomes transparent,

and that all the secrets of God's Word can become clear to us.

The first day you read the Bible, you are blind in it; but the

more times you

read it, the more God will reveal Himself to you.

The more you go to church, the more community and

Christianity is revealed to

you.

There are many out there who do not recognize Jesus and

denounce Him as

God our Lord. Why?

Because they do not know Him

There are many who do not recognize God and will turn

their back on Him,

and turn away in a heartbeat.

There are many who push away the Holy Spirit and will

erratically deny

The Holy Spirits

existence.

But when the Lord reveals Himself to you, you will know.

You will see Him working in your life,

and there will be no way you can turn away and lie to

yourself.

God lives now; He has been here since before there was

light, before the earth

was formed, for He is the Word the "I Am"

He has been the overseer of all humankind since the

beginning of

humanity's

existence.

He is in the present to all who come with humble hearts.

He is in the future, and there is no stopping God;

just like I said, the Father, the Son, and the Holy Spirit are

three persons

and one in essence.

So Jesus is the Son, but the Son is of the Father, who is God,

and they are one and of the Holy Spirit.

They are one together, and one never contradicts each

other.

They are separate but working together,

and they are as one together in existence.

And the Trinity is sovereign over the earth and all that the

earth has on and in it.

The Trinity, which is the Father, the Son and the Holy

Spirit, is fully sovereign

within the heavenly realms

and even hell and its desolate places.

The meaning of sovereign is as follows:

supreme in power and authority;

having independent authority and

a power to govern without external control.

Holy Bible

(NIV®.) John 6:44 New International Version (NIV)

[44] "No one can come to me unless the Father who sent me draws them, and I will raise them up at the last day.

*

So Jesus is God incarnate.

He will disclose Himself to the humble, the Gentile, the different, the mild,

the withdrawn, the fearful, the obedient, the tentative, the meek, the poor,

the needy, the broken, and the lost.

God gives His grace to the humble at heart

because He turns away from the proud,

and reveals Himself to the humble at heart,

that we may become His people,

and rely on His Grace and be

His adopted children. "Amen!" Praises to the Lord.

A RELATIONSHIP IN CHRIST

Book 3

7

This book is almost over, and I am proud of you for hearing

these words

and taking them in and allowing them to cultivate your spirit,

for I want you to succeed in life

and be a bright and shining star with the Holy Spirit,

that everyone may know that you are under the Lord's

saving grace.

Peace be with you.

Here are some more of my favourites:

Holy Bible

(NIV®.) Matthew 10:26-28 New International Version (NIV)

[26] "So do not be afraid of them, for there is nothing

concealed that will not be disclosed, or hidden that will not

be made known. [27] What I tell you in the dark, speak in the

daylight; what is whispered in your ear, proclaim from the

roofs. [28] Do not be afraid of those who kill the body but

cannot kill the soul. Rather, be afraid of the One who can destroy both soul and body in hell.

*

Holy Bible

(NIV®.) Matthew 10:32-33 New International Version (NIV)

[32] "Whoever acknowledges me before others, I will also acknowledge before my Father in heaven. [33] But whoever disowns me before others, I will disown before my Father in heaven.

*

Holy Bible

(NIV®.)Matthew 10:38-39 New International Version (NIV)

[38] Whoever does not take up their cross and follow me is not worthy of me. [39] Whoever finds their life will lose it, and whoever loses their life for my sake will find it.

✱

Holy Bible

(NIV®.) Matthew 10:40 New International Version (NIV)

40 "Anyone who welcomes you welcomes me, and anyone who welcomes me welcomes the one who sent me.

✱

Holy Bible

(NIV®.) 2 Corinthians 13:9-10 New International Version (NIV)

9 We are glad whenever we are weak but you are strong; and our prayer is that you may be fully restored. 10 This is why I write these things when I am absent, that when I come I may not have to be harsh in my use of authority—the authority the Lord gave me for building you up, not for tearing you down.

Book 3

8

God bless you all.

May your life go well.

Do not lose this moment in time,

for I hope you have been enlightened

and enjoy your relationship with the Lord.

Jesus is His name.

We Are Close

Poem Book 3

9

Lord, I love you so,

for You have taken a hold of my life

and You're never letting go.

As I hold on by faith, I as well am never letting go.

By Your love, You bring me up high,

for I am never low.

We are one, and spiritually we flow.

I have faith that I will always be with You, Lord Jesus,

for we are one, and we will never give up or let go,

for we are one mind, body and soul,

and the heavens above will it so.

Thank You, Lord, for coming into my life,

for You have forgiven me and washed the stains of my sins

white as snow.

In my past I wish I had received Your saving grace,

for in my life I needed it years ago.

Life could have gone different for me,

but, Lord, I may never know.

A RELATIONSHIP IN CHRIST

Book 3

10

From non-existence to the existence,

all existence started from God's Word,

for His Word caused existence.

From God's Word, all creation was formed,

for God is almighty and powerful.

We are carnal people initially without spirituality,

for we are merely human, humanistic and temporal.

Through our nature, we are even against entertaining the

thought of God,

for our hearts are completely worldly within the place of

our godly wants,

needs and desires,

for we are all unusually far from God;

and knowing Him is in the back of our minds,

but He reveals Himself to us.

Before we see Him working in our lives, it is hard for us to

comprehend Him,

but it is even written in the Bible that only a fool denies

God, for in that person's

defense, he or she will say that God does not exist.

Holy Bible

(NIV®.) Psalm 24:1 New International Version (NIV)

¹ The earth is the Lord's, and everything in it,

the world, and all who live in it;

For people scheme against God,

they plot evil within their hearts

and laugh at the believer.

The non-believer plots to deceive the Christian's heart,

but the believer has seen the Lord working within

his or her life,

for the believer gives the Lord great reverence, with deep

respect and awe,

for the Lord is our Saviour; He alone we worship,

for God is worthy.

So when you worship give God admiration, high esteem,

honour, and you're love

Worship through your spirit, with your devotion, loyalty,

and awe struck

wonder nearby.

When you wholeheartedly worship, you can honestly see

God's position

as our Mighty God and Father of Heaven.

He is a friend to the friendless,

a father to the fatherless,

a gentle hand to the widow

and a guiding light to a child;

He is a brother to the lonely at heart,

He is an advocate to the innocent and accused,

He is the overseer to the poor, hungry and homeless and to

the one in need.

But He is not a buddy; He is not there to talk about

baseball or the hockey game.

He's not there to give you pointers on the horse race,

for He is pure in mind and pure in heart and above all

humanity.

He's not a man who will keep you out of jail when charged

with a legit offence

or manipulate the system by breaking the law,

but He is a God whom you can talk to intimately,

who will hear your case and your please.

He will hear your prayers for other's needs and your prayers

for your needs.

He might not give you all your earthly desires, but He will

give you your needs.

Just ask and you shall receive.

He is just, and He will clear the names of the innocent.

He will be an advocate to the broken in spirit.

If you have done a crime, indeed you will go to jail.

Just pray that the Lord looks after you there.

For He is omnipresent, He is there at all time in all places.

Pray that He will watch over you, and keep your hands

clean that your life may go

well,

for what I'm trying to say is that God is above all humanity.

His thoughts are above all.

His mind is above all.

His actions are above all.

His heart is above all.

His plans are above all,

and His will for us is above all humanity's comprehension.

For He is pure and without flaw, there is none who can

compare to Him

in Glory and in Power. Amen.

He knows all, sees all, and is in all places at all times.

For He is the Creator, His foundation is secure.

There is no shaking Him, for He is established;

and His throne will endure forever.

Whether you believe it or not, God has power over all

creation,

but He has instilled free will within us;

but no matter how free we think we are,

we're continuously slaves to sin.

Without Jesus, we are powerless in fighting sin

and helpless from being forgiven of our sins;

and this makes us separate from God.

We are in bondage to sin and a slave of sin,

but we do have free will to believe in God or not,

for the Lord does not wish to see us perish in sin and die for

our sins,

for sin is in control of us, for that is why God gave us His

Son,

that we may be saved from sin.

Jesus died on the cross for our sins, and through His death

and resurrection,

whoever believes and whoever comes

to Jesus Christ is justified

and pardoned.

When sin is removed, we are pronounced and credited

blameless

and righteous in God's eyes.

The Lord hears our prayers; He is steadfast in love and well

established.

He alone is the giver of faith,

so I tell you, do not turn on Him or let Him down, for

your salvation is at stake.

Allow Him to work His faith in you like yeast in dough;

be loyal in your life to God;

fix your heart on God.

For the First Commandment is that you shall have no other

god before Him,

you are to love God with all your heart, mind,

strength and soul.

So be steadfast in your love for the Lord;

offer Him your unwavering love.

Use the faith that you have received from Him to do deeds

by faith

through the power of the Holy Spirit.

Use the grace He has given you wisely, for as a believer you
are already saved and
that you may glorify Him in all you do.
Worship the Lord day and night through song,
through giving, through learning, through teaching,
through introducing children to Jesus as well as the old.
Glorify God by becoming more active in the church, by
finding your place;
read and learn about the Lord and all He stands for,
that you will use it in your life, by replicating Jesus and
recognizing Him.
Do not idolize anything else or worship anything else besides
the God of Israel whose Son's name is Jesus, the Jesus of
Nazareth,
for our God is a jealous God.
Only God's son, Jesus Christ, can alter God's wrath.
So work with Jesus so that you will be defined as upright in
heart.
Listen to your heart.
For obedience is to the wise, there is no age linked to the
meaning of obedience,
but great knowledge, wisdom and understanding pertains
to it.

In life, there is only two ways a person can go:

One, people will not accept God in their lives and turn

from Him and run

away from God,

and even hide from His powerful presence.

It might be that all these people see is

judgment.

Or two, you will accept God and all His fullness; you will

allow Him to draw you in.

You will become a part of His life, as He will become a part

of your life.

For in its fullness, it becomes a relationship, and you both

share life in unity,

fellowship and communion together,

for, as believers, your response to God is through worship,

A vital aspect of all believers' lives is to know the bible,

listen to the bible,

read the bible,

pray the bible,

sing the bible,

and preach the bible.

God's word is the Holy bible. God's word is the means of

your new birth

For it is written for further growth and instruction.

So sing praises to the Lord, because salvation belongs to the

Lord.

Some see Jesus as weak, but they mistake kindness for

weakness, for the Lord was

a manly carpenter.

He would walk for days at a time along

rough terrain in His sandals.

He could resist all temptation, even from the devil himself.

He came with great authority.

He fought all opposition, all the Pharisees who sought

to take His life,

He brought down by His tongue; His words were like a

double-edged sword.

He even had the power and strength to face

the day of His own murder,

which He knew in advance since the beginning of time.

He was beaten half to death and picked up His cross, and

He walked with it

to His death.

His death was not capital punishment for

a crime or an offence,

for He was innocent and blameless and

without sin.

God came down to be in flesh. He is Jesus, God incarnate.

He came in the formed as a man.

He was a man filled with power. He will forever be known

to the people

as Emmanuel. "God with us"

For the most important thing is love,

and love for all of God's creation.

There is no stopping God; He is like a blazing fire. There is

no end,

for He is Everlasting to Everlasting.

The purpose of singing should be of great importance to

the believer.

It is a way to give worship to the Lord.

It is our offering to the Lord.

May you be prepared within your heart

and mind.

That you're offering of worship may be pleasing to the Lord

that we can look at Him with adoration

pay Him honour through divine worship.

Give Him homage, give Him high regard, and give Him

great esteem,

for there is no one like Him.

When you sing for Him, sing with fervent passion and devotion.

Show the Lord your love by your intensity of spirit; give Him your enthusiasm,

for the Lord loves a cheerful heart.

Sing, sing and sing to the heavens above,

for you are under the protection of God. Amen!

With all your might, live with a faithful heart and worship with loyalty.

Do not be distracted, for life has its own problems, I know;

but remember why you are worshipping the Lord.

It is to acknowledge God

for His salvation, for building up the churches, for forgiving us our sin,

for helping us in all we do,

for feeding us, for giving us shelter, for being a refuge, for giving joy to the sad,

for helping us fight all sin, for being a good Father and for loving us.

It's a way to show Him that we love Him and respect Him.

It is a way to bring honour to Him and to acknowledge that we honour Him.

Look to the Lord with fear and trembling, for our lives are

in His hands alone,

our salvation is in His hands alone,

our future is in His hands alone,

our resurrection is in His hands alone,

our day of judgment is in His hands alone.

Fear of the Lord is to the obedient,

for one needs to have a high view of God.

For this is wise,

one needs to continuously repent for sin, whether it be a sin

of omission or

commission.

Omission of sin is when one is aware of a good or right

thing that one

should do but fails to do.

God's will or Word in one's life is being neglected or has

been neglected.

There might be something left out or not done.

Commission of sin is a specific act.

Sin that's willfully chosen, that is forbidden by God,

contrasts with the sin of omission.

Because with omission of sin it is to neglect from doing

good things

which is for performing acts and the avoidance of harm to the heart, mind, body, and soul.

Commission is the awareness of sin and the willingness to commit sin

or head in the direction of sin.

To get ready to worship, remember whomever you have bad blood with forgive that person or persons,

that when you worship, your heart may be calm and open to the Lord.

Do not do anything throughout the week that will not be resolved by the day of the Sabbath.

If you have a problem of any kind, do not let sleep come to your eyes until your problem is resolved;

this is a true remark and a wise one to live by.

Forgive and be forgiven and resolve your problems.

Forgive and you will be forgiven, for forgiveness and the power to forgive comes from our Father's Grace.

Do not let anything block your path to worship.

The days before the Sabbath you should be preparing

your tidings, your

outer wear as well as your inner ware,

like your hearts and your souls,

for the Third Commandment says thou shall keep the

Sabbath day Holy.

Just as I have said, worship for Christians is most important.

One should look forward to the day of the Lord, for it is a

day to rest from all work

a day to worship the Lord, to learn and to listen to His Word,

for we come to share in community and communion with

the Lord and

other believers.

For it is a day set aside for our Lord,

it is a Holy day for our Saviour;

so make sure you keep every Sabbath of the week Holy.

I hope that you look

at God with awe

and worship with bright hearts and praising tongues, for

our Lord, and Saviour

is worthy of all Praise.

Amen.

A RELATIONSHIP IN CHRIST

Book 3

11

If you're a true Christian, you cannot be slothful and

zealous at the same

time,

for you can be only one.

Just like the believer's heart,

it's either zealous for God or it is slothful and inactive.

We all come through the same gate;

it is the door to everlasting life and it is only acquired

through Jesus,

by being zealous in knowing, loving and serving God.

For there is no fast track to know God,

do not become a sidetracked servant.

We need to become fired up for the Lord.

Everyone has zeal for something. What are you zealous for?

Sin, self-indulgence or things of the world; for money,

work, sex or academics?

God's Word brings instruction, encouragement and

edification.

Love, know and serve God.

Be zealous and passionate;

do not be cold or disconnected from God.

Love God and all His creations.

If you do not have God in your life, you cannot teach about

God or godly things.

There are only two kinds of people:

the sheep and the goat;

the believer, who is saved,

and the non-believer, who is under the law and is

condemned;

the redeemed and the unregenerate.

We as humans have imagined three types of people:

believers, non-believers, and people who think they are

believers

But the third group of people is not zealous for God;

they might come to church, but they do not know God,

for they do not have an intimate relationship with God.

Throughout the week, they're busy with life and

may leave the Lord on the back burner and forget about

Him easily.

They do not talk about Him with their friends or family,

not to mention strangers.

They do not profess His name or His good works to the

people.

They do not greet Jesus in the morning or talk to Him

throughout the day.

They do not pray to God at their meals, like Jesus did.

They do not pray for others, and they rob them of a blessing.

And when they lay their heads at night, they rob themselves

of their own blessing

because

they do not pray.

They have not found time for God and neglect Him,

and they have little faith, for they need a sign to believe,

for they easily forget what the Lord has done for them.

They are on the fence, and may never see God.

I pray this is not you; I pray you have an intimate

relationship with Jesus our Lord

on a daily basis.

I pray you can see God's empathy, love and compassion.

When you get to know God, you will see He is not all

about sin and the wrong

we do.

It's about love in communion and loving, trusting,

defending and respecting

one another.

Days are more fulfilling when you spend them with God

just getting to know

Him

and being together.

Be enlightened; just try and get to know our Father in

heaven better

and see for yourself.

Life's worries just fade away into the background

and things become clearer

and sin becomes less appealing and easier to

turn away from.

Pray for peace on every side. I did, and I know the Lord

will not give me anything

that I cannot handle.

So glorify God, for even the food you eat and all the money

you spend came from

God. So be good stewards

and help everyone in need.

Love one another to the fullest of the meaning.

Worship God in all you do and have a
relationship with Him,
like it was your last day, like you would be face-to-face
with the Lord by the
day's end.
Everyone has sinned and falls short of the Glory of God.
We need righteousness, how can we receive it?
We can only acquire it from God; He is the provider
through His Son Jesus.
Our righteousness has been manifested through our faith
in Jesus.
The gospel teaches us how to acquire righteousness.
For it comes from Jesus and His death and resurrection,
we are reconciled to God
from our belief in His Son Jesus.
Through Jesus, we are able to live a life in Christ, we
become righteous by His
righteousness,
we become brothers and sisters in Christ we are people
under His refuge made blameless.
When I say our sins I mean the believer.

For in our world it is plain to see that there is

no shortage of zeal for idols?

But we need to be fervent and boiling over with zeal for

God our Lord,

for God loves a

steadfast, patient, loyal, devoted and zealous Christian.

Holy Bible

(NIV®.) Galatians 5:16-21 New International Version (NIV)

[16] So I say, walk by the Spirit, and you will not gratify the

desires of the flesh. [17] For the flesh desires what is contrary

to the Spirit, and the Spirit what is contrary to the flesh.

They are in conflict with each other, so that you are not to

do whatever[a] you want. [18] But if you are led by the Spirit,

you are not under the law.

[19] The acts of the flesh are obvious: sexual immorality,

impurity and debauchery; [20] idolatry and witchcraft; hatred,

discord, jealousy, fits of rage, selfish ambition, dissensions,

factions [21] and envy; drunkenness, orgies, and the like. I

warn you, as I did before, that those who live like this will

not inherit the kingdom of God.

Holy Bible

(NIV®.) Galatians 5:22-26 New International Version (NIV)

²² But the fruit of the Spirit is love, joy, peace, forbearance, kindness, goodness, faithfulness, ²³ gentleness and self-control. Against such things there is no law. ²⁴ Those who belong to Christ Jesus have crucified the flesh with its passions and desires. ²⁵ Since we live by the Spirit, let us keep in step with the Spirit. ²⁶ Let us not become conceited, provoking and envying each other.

We like cold or hot water and have no need for lukewarm.

For this depiction is just like our zeal for God and for our belief in the Lord,

work to keep your pot boiling hot, not cold, and expressly not lukewarm,

for there is no purpose for lukewarm.

To be on the fence with one foot in and one foot out or dishonestly loving God,

for I tell you He knows all hearts and minds.

He is a God who tests hearts, for He is forever seeking the truth.

If you are lukewarm in your Christian life,

I pray that your fire be rekindled, rebuilt or even stocked,

for your treasures are stored up in heaven and

the Lord's inheritance on earth for it is here and now.

Commit to the Lord and have it shown in all the glory you

give to the Lord.

Share His word that people may know His glory and seek

His grace,

that people

may see it working in your life and through your hands.

The heart is an idol-making machine, and it never stops.

The mind continually unravels idols to worship.

Together they are forever creating idols

to pull us further from what really matters in life—

God!

One shall never bow down or worship an idol of any kind,

in any way.

Be wise, because this will invoke anger in the Lord,

for we all have our boiling point.

Do not have a religious conviction or point of view when

being zealous for the

Lord.

We are to have a true and honest relationship with Him.

Know Him, love Him, trust Him, rely on Him, defend

Him, have fellowship with

Him, give thanks offerings to Him.

We are to have a relationship with Him like a father

has to a son or daughter.

He is our good Father,

unlike most of our worldly fathers.

He is slow to anger, just, merciful, forgiving, patient,

honest, truthful, loving,

compassionate, trustworthy and praiseworthy.

If you are a believer and you are getting cold or lukewarm

in spirit,

go back to the beginning. Remember when you were fallen.

Do you recall?

Do you remember when you first came to the Lord?

Do you remember how you were on fire for Him?

Do you remember when you could not get enough,

when you were starving for His Word?

Well, go back to that day, to the day you first believed.

Start at the beginning of the path when you gave your heart

to the Lord.

Pray and pray hard,

and remember all the things you did, like reading the Bible,

going to church,

praying,

worshipping, singing,

feeling certain and secure in life;

or the times you sat and just spent time talking to God.

So from the bottom of my heart,

I hope I have not been too prolix.

I am going to confide in you and tell you that being a

Christian is not always easy.

But the Lord gives joy to us in the hardest of times.

The walk with Jesus is very rewarding

but not always easy.

Throughout the Christian's life, there will be great rewards

and immense accomplishments will happen.

Discipline is evident in the life of the believer,

and structure comes with obedience and is acquired by God's

wisdom, knowledge and understanding.

Please be filled with joy and pray without ceasing;

be relaxed when you are getting to know Christ.

May the Lord give you motivation.

Amen. May all our energy be used to serve the Lord our God.

Jesus is His name.

John 17:1-30 New International Version (NIV)

Jesus Prays to Be Glorified

17 After Jesus said this, he looked toward heaven and prayed: "Father, the hour has come. Glorify your Son, that your Son may glorify you. ² For you granted him authority over all people that he might give eternal life to all those you have given him. ³ Now this is eternal life: that they know you, the only true God, and Jesus Christ, whom you have sent. ⁴ I have brought you glory on earth by finishing the work you gave me to do. ⁵ And now, Father, glorify me in your presence with the glory I had with you before the world began.

Jesus Prays for His Disciples

⁶ "I have revealed you[a] to those whom you gave me out of the world. They were yours; you gave them to me and they have obeyed your word. ⁷ Now they know that everything you have given me comes from you. ⁸ For I gave them the words you gave me and they accepted them. They knew with certainty that I came from you, and they believed that you sent me. ⁹ I pray for them. I am not praying for the world, but for those you have given me, for they are yours. ¹⁰ All I have is yours, and all you have is mine. And glory

has come to me through them. [11] I will remain in the world no longer, but they are still in the world, and I am coming to you. Holy Father, protect them by the power of your name, the name you gave me, so that they may be one as we are one. [12] While I was with them, I protected them and kept them safe by that name you gave me. None has been lost except the one doomed to destruction so that Scripture would be fulfilled.

[13] "I am coming to you now, but I say these things while I am still in the world, so that they may have the full measure of my joy within them. [14] I have given them your word and the world has hated them, for they are not of the world any more than I am of the world. [15] My prayer is not that you take them out of the world but that you protect them from the evil one. [16] They are not of the world, even as I am not of it. [17] Sanctify them by the truth; your word is truth. [18] As you sent me into the world, I have sent them into the world. [19] For them I sanctify myself, that they too may be truly sanctified.

Jesus Prays for All Believers

[20] "My prayer is not for them alone. I pray also for those who will believe in me through their message, [21] that all of them may be one, Father, just as you are in me and I am in

you. May they also be in us so that the world may believe that you have sent me. ²² I have given them the glory that you gave me, that they may be one as we are one—²³ I in them and you in me—so that they may be brought to complete unity. Then the world will know that you sent me and have loved them even as you have loved me.

²⁴ "Father, I want those you have given me to be with me where I am, and to see my glory, the glory you have given me because you loved me before the creation of the world. ²⁵ "Righteous Father, though the world does not know you, I know you, and they know that you have sent me. ²⁶ I have made you known to them, and will continue to make you known in order that the love you have for me may be in them and that I myself may be in them."